STALKED

MY STORY OF TERROR AND TRIUMPH

MARION LANGLI

This publication is designed to provide informative and useful information regarding the subject matter covered. However, it is sold with the understanding that the author and publisher are not engaged in rendering legal, financial, or other professional advice. Laws and practices vary from country to country and state to state. If legal or other expert assistance is required, the services of a professional should be sought.

The author and the publisher specifically disclaim any liability that is incurred from the use or application of the contents of this book.

REACHABEL FUTURES PRESS
Helping You Unlock Your Potential

First Edition, First Printing – Copyright © 2024 by Reachabel Futures Press. All rights reserved under International and Pan-American Copyright Conventions. No part of this book may be reproduced in any form or by any means, electronic or mechanical, including photocopying, without permission in writing from the publisher. All inquiries should be addressed to Reachabel Futures Press - abel@reachabel.com

Cover design by Debraj
Layout by Lilian
Edited by Sean Thomas
Front & back cover photo by Marcus Leveau
ISBN 979-8-9902166-0-0

Acknowledgements

There are many people surrounding me whom I want to express my heartfelt gratitude to. I would like to express my appreciation to Dr. Denis Cauvier and his team for their guidance in writing my first book. Denis has been with me every step of the way, answering questions and guiding me. He made me see that I had the ability to accomplish this.

I'm deeply grateful to my dear friend Svein Østvik, who through his example of perseverance has become a vital presence in my life. His unwavering support and encouragement helped me find strength in the toughest of times.

I also want to thank Marcus Leveau for donating his time and talent in creating the photographs for the book's front and back cover. He is such a great photographer and his work is amazing. Over the years, he has become a close friend.

I'd like to thank Marcus' family for opening their home to me in some of the scariest times in Mallorca as I tried to establish my new life.

I am grateful to my boyfriend, Abel, for his support in helping me put my thoughts on paper, and always pushing me forward. I am forever grateful for his way of understanding.

I am so grateful to my family for their constant support, for always doing their best with me even through tough times. Despite everything I've put them through, they have always had my back.

I want to thank my cousin Ylva for being my closest friend throughout my life. She is always honest, supportive, and caring. Additionally, she's the one who asks important questions to ensure my well-being.

I want to thank my friend Anette. She came through when I needed it the most. She helped me get out of the situation I was in by giving me the courage to act. I don't know where things would have gone without her showing up at the most critical moment of my life.

My friend Bjarne in Oslo deserves my heartfelt thanks. He graciously opened his home to me and my cat, making sure we were taken care of.

I would like to express my gratitude to my dear friend Raymond, whom I met while in Drammen. Without hesitation, he gladly provided me with a place to stay when I needed it once more. He is one of the kindest people I have ever met, and I feel incredibly fortunate to have him in my life.

Finally, I'm forever grateful to the Spanish Guardia Civil for their assistance, and I want to acknowledge their contribution. They brought back a sense of hope that I had lost.

Dedication

This book is dedicated to all those who have been victims of stalking. To everyone who has ever experienced being ignored, let down, or ignored by the system, this book is for you.

To all those out there who feel alone and helpless but still fight on, this book is for you.

I have written this book in honour of those that are too scared to speak out and seek the help they need.

This book is further dedicated to those who are no longer here and are unable to share their own particular real-life horror stories.

I became motivated to write this book in order to not only tell my own particular story, but as an attempt to give a voice to anyone out there who is crying out for help, but not receiving the crucial attention they require to stay safe.

The anger, frustration, and sadness I feel for the many victims killed by their stalkers also fuels my motivation.

And finally, this book is dedicated to all the friends and families who are left behind wondering, "Why?"

Table of Contents

Personal Message from the Author 6

Introduction 7

Chapter 1: Early Years 9

Chapter 2: Experiences 13

Chapter 3: A Friend Across the Street 24

Chapter 4: The Nightmare Descends 32

Chapter 5: New life, New Country 63

Chapter 6: Aftershock 66

Chapter 7: Writing the Future 77

Conclusion: Embracing Resilience 80

Resources 82

Safety Plan for Victims of Stalking 85

Online Stalker Victim Resources 92

Personal Message from the Author

Dear Reader,

Sharing the intimate details of my journey surviving a stalker leaves me humbled and hopeful. I strongly believe that sharing my personal experience of going from fear and despair to triumph can help shed light on the widespread problem of stalking and give a voice to silent victims.

This book is more than just a recounting of events; it is a testament to the strength of the human spirit, the power of resilience, and the unwavering support that comes from those who stand with us.

Stalking is a complex and insidious crime that affects countless lives. By sharing my story, I hope to promote understanding and compassion and break the isolation that often comes with such traumatic experiences. If a single person discovers solace in realizing they're not alone, then this journey will have been worthwhile.

In these pages, you'll bear witness to an unfiltered story of survival, a testament to the strength of friendship and family bonds, as well a naiive young woman seeking the determination to restore a sense of security to her shattered life. I want to shine a light on the scourge of stalking, and promote a sense of resilience, courage, and a shared determination to create tangible change.

As we navigate this narrative together, let us remember that stories have the power to heal, to educate, and to create empathy. I hope my journey can be a source of inspiration for others who face similar paths to mine and assure them that there is hope, assistance, and a community that will embrace them.

Thank you for accompanying me on this journey of personal growth. May the pages ahead bring awareness, understanding, and ultimately, the strength to stand tall against the shadows that seek to engulf us.

With gratitude and hope,

Marion Langli

Introduction

Imagine this: I was at home with two of my friends. We were convinced the men who had been stalking and tormenting me for months were outside my home watching us. Rick, my trusted friend and roommate, received chilling messages that instructed him to go outside and "sacrifice" himself for me. I was unsure what "sacrifice" meant—did it mean he would be killed or kidnapped? It felt surreal, like a scene straight out of a horror film.

We were coldly informed that our every move was under surveillance. Seeking safety from the predators, we all lay down flat on the floor to in order to avoid being seen through any window and potentially even shot at.

The surreal demand left us all in a state of panic and disbelief. Rick, convinced that he needed to comply in order to protect me, began preparing to go outside, ready to face an ominous fate. He was crying uncontrollably. We all were. Witnessing my friend's emotional breakdown and facing the prospect of something terrible happening to him shook me to my core. Desperation set in as we contemplated the unthinkable scenario unfolding before us.

Fearing for our lives, we decided to call the police although we had been instructed by the tormentors not to do so. While waiting for them to arrive, more panic set in. Rick remained determined to go outside and sacrifice himself. I tried to stop him by jumping on top of him. Anette was sobbing right beside us. The wait seemed endless, as the seconds and minutes stretched into hours. Was this the end? Was tonight the night we were going to die?

The situation that I just described probably seems very dark and confusing to you, but as I take you through my story you will see how things developed into such a nightmarish situation.

Before going any further, you may be wondering who I am. I'm the girl next door. The ordinary girl you meet at the supermarket getting her groceries, or sitting next to you on the bus. I could be your sister. I could be your daughter.

With this book I invite you to delve into a pervasive crisis that transcends geographical borders and societal norms. Through these pages, my own terrifying journey is revealed—an experience that dragged me through the dangerous world of stalking and eventually led me to uncover the worldwide evil that affects countless lives around the world.

The aim of my book is more than simply to tell my own personal and terrifying story, it is to serve as a warning to others and raise awareness of this growing and global problem. The statistics presented here are more than just numbers; they are cold hard facts detailing the scope of a problem that is often hiding in plain sight.

CHAPTER 1
Early Years

Wanting Approval

My early years were a comfortable and very happy time growing up in a small town in central Norway. I loved the outdoors, running around the local woods and swimming in one of the many lakes, but most of all I enjoyed our close family ties and the general sense of security you can only really experience as a child.

I enjoyed kindergarten, but it was at times, a bit of a challenge. My fellow kindergarteners were very bossy. These two friends of mine, the puppet masters of my childhood, never let me call the shots. From choosing our games to deciding our hangout spots, I felt my say didn't count. Their influence extended to the lunch menu—I would often ask my mother to prepare my meals based on their preferences. Our association extended past kindergarten; we rode the same school bus until I was five or six. Even after one of them took a different school route, their affect on me still remained. I hungered for their stamp of approval—a desperate craving to fit in, to get that nod of acceptance.

Reflecting on my early years, I now understand the reasons behind my early behavioral problems. Flashbacks of one of those buddies dismissing my every move as silly or weird came rushing back to me. To this day, I can still vividly recall the skeptical expressions on their faces as they questioned my every decision. They made me feel so different, out of place, and I started to question my own authenticity. Those moments, and their faces, linger on in my memory to this day. It wasn't their fault. They were just kids. Who knows what they were going through to make them act that way towards me.

These early years set the stage, laying the foundation for a relentless pursuit of approval and a hunger for acceptance. Two issues that would continue to shape my life.

Pressure

I was raised in a world of professional athletes. My father is a world famous Olympic gold medalist who is a legend in cross-country skiing. My mother was the undisputed champion of the local cross-country scene, and holds two gold medals from the Norwegian national championship. Now, imagine the backdrop since I was knee-high: at every family gathering, every friend's visit, the same chorus echoed—"Here comes the next superstar, the future Olympic champion!" It's not that it was a bad thing to hear. I understood it; I was born into this environment, but sometimes it became overwhelming.

From an early age, I started to feel like I could never measure up, the constant weight of expectation hung over me like a relentless storm cloud. Skiing, once about the exhilaration of the wind and speed, became a chore and a space for judgment. I'd hit the slopes, and instead of just enjoying the ride, I felt persistent pressure. Eventually, in the middle of the local ski competition, I tossed away my skis put my arms up and said, "No more."

That was a tipping point in my childhood, but it didn't stop there. This baggage, this suffocating pressure to excel, followed me to school. I tried out for all the team sports – but soon discovered they were not my strong suit. Instead of giving it a proper shot, I'd recoil. Competitions? No thanks. The pressure turned every attempt into a grand performance, and I just wanted out. It became this overbearing force which dictated what I could or couldn't enjoy, shaping my choices under the constant weight of expectation.

Looking for An Alternative

Growing up in the countryside, I was irresistibly drawn to the nearby stable at a very early age. In fact, by the age of 5 years old, I had become a familiar face around there. I eagerly volunteered to help out with all the different chores, just to be in the company of those magnificent horses. Despite not having my own horse, I experienced a great sense of fulfillment in taking care of the stable horses. This experience instilled in me a deep sense of responsibility, empathy, and general sense of decency. As time passed, my skills and understanding of horses continued to improve, and I felt a profound sense of belonging. It was a remarkable feeling to excel in something I was truly passionate about.

Every night, I would return home and dream of owning my very own horse one day. I devoted myself to studying books, watching films, and seeking guidance from people who knew far more than me, in order to expand my own knowledge. At the age of 11 I got my first horse, a little Norwegian pony called Pinky. She became my world, and while going through my struggles socially and at school, she would always be there to comfort me. Eventually, my parents helped me move her to my uncle's farm, just a few minutes from our house. It was a great feeling to have her so close and she provided me with endless hours of joy and emotional support.

Lack of confidence and self-esteem are the consequences of a complicated chain of experiences. Fear of failure haunted me as I went through life day after day. I was terrified to meet new people. What would they think of me? It was a relentless loop in my head; and my mother noticed it too. There came a point where I was almost afraid of people. Even with close family friends or relatives—it didn't matter. I'd shy away from conversations, terrified of the judgment I might face. There was this constant worry that my words, my actions, would never be good enough.

As the storm clouds gathered, other people began noticing changes in my behaviour too. During my pre-teen years, new friends led to new expectations from more people. It was like a spotlight on my imperfections. It reached a stage where I mentally disconnected from school, distanced myself from friends, and isolated myself from any situation in which I might be uncomfortable. My inner struggles persisted.

As a protective response, my brain attempted to distance itself. I've come to understand that this mental barrier I've constructed is a way to protect myself. If any thoughts and experiences are linked to pain, the brain instinctively creates separate rooms, storage spaces, to dump it all in. It's like building a fortress and slapping a hefty lock on it, in an attempt to keep me safe. Remembering becomes a challenge because the brain's shouting, "No, we put up a wall, and we're keeping it locked for your own protection."

During the process of slowly breaking down these walls, some memories I hadn't thought about for years resurfaced. I've tried to take a disciplined approach to this, and tell myself, "I'm okay, I'm an adult, let's unpack this and learn from it." This experience has been emotional and revealing, connecting the dots and shedding light on the problems I faced growing up.

Looking back, it's like I'm not simply recalling my earlier years; I'm seeing a frightened little girl, and, honestly, I feel sorry for her. As an adult, it's peculiar—it's almost like I'm peering into someone else's story, detached from all the emotional weight. I think the solution lies in having objectivity, as well as the tools, experience, and maturity to approach past experiences logically and derive meaningful insights.

CHAPTER 2
Experiences

Wanting Acceptance

The start of middle school felt like an opportuntity for a fresh start. Although I felt scared, it was a chance to rewrite the narrative that had been haunting me for far too long.

When I was 12, I was a bit nervous about starting middle school but on the one hand I was excited to meet new people. I began to explore other friendships. I was searching for a group where I could be myself and find acceptance. After a while, I managed to find a group of outsiders similar to me, and it felt amazing to finally belong.

Despite my joy at having found a group of people with whom I could relate to, some of my new friends faced challenges of their own, such as with substance abuse, broken families, and other less than ideal situations for teenagers. Despite this, I felt overjoyed to have finally come across individuals who accepted me as myself, and I was eager to embrace new adventures.

Growing up in a small Norwegian town, as a teenager I longed to explore the world beyond the boundaries of the familiar. One of the advantages of living in such a small town however, is that age restrictions weren't strictly enforced, so the pursuit of adolescent thrills mainly involved getting alcohol and a car, and hosting a mobile party. This served as my entry point into the world of "substance experimentation." Little did I know at the time, that this was a path that would later lead to terrible consequences for myself and others.

Drugs and Bathrooms

One such consequence would change my life forever — a rendezvous with a friend and an unfamiliar substance in a school restroom. It was a morning like any other morning. My friend and I met up at the bus stop close to school so we could chat and hang out before heading in for class. Feeling adventurous, we decided to accept a spontaneous invitation from a mutual friend of ours who said he had something he wanted us to try. Naively we enthusiastically headed to the bathroom to take him up on the offer. We split the powder between the two of us, but my friend couldn't do all of hers so I ended up finishing my friend's half as well. Well if some is good, more is better, I thought.

What began as a bit of harmless fun swiftly escalated into a surreal nightmare. After I had sniffed the strange powder, the world around me began to disintegrate, and I found myself grappling with an altered reality. In a state of desperation, I literally crawled my way to the counsellor's office, seeking help as my mind disconnected from my body.

The following few hours unfolded in a confusing and disorienting patchwork—a trip to the police station, surreal visions, and an unsettling encounter with the authorities. My friend and I were separated for interrogation. After a while, we were taken to the nearby emergency room for a medical check over.

The doctor's visit is still all a big blur. I wasn't really able to communicate. My mother showed up in a state of shock. I didn't recognize her. In my head she looked like a man with a long beard who was dressed like a pirate. I also made a really deep connection with a plant in the waiting room. It was a dinosaur plant and he was my friend.

My mother and I went back to the police station for another round of interrogation. By this time, I was finally able to communicate somewhat clearly. However, the detective attempting to question me kept being bombarded by pieces of my chewing gum that I kept throwing her way. Every time I looked at her I thought she was crying. So I would repeatedly ask her if she was okay. After a few hours of this "interrogation" my mother took me home, where we had a long and meaningful heart-to-heart.

Looking back on it, I am very grateful for both my parents' reaction to the whole ordeal. I felt stupid, but my parents' willingness to be there for me without judgment or condemnation was vital, even though it was a very shameful situation. I will be forever grateful for all the love and support they showed me at that moment in my life – I needed it.

My friend and I were both suspended from school. Not only that but we made it into the local newspaper because the substance was later identified as 2C-E, a psychedelic drug similar to LSD that had made its way into this small town for the first time. The whole town now knew what we had done. From then on we were both labelled as the bad kids in town. All our other friends' parents didn't let them hang out with us anymore. We were completely ostracized. There were persistent rumors going around town that we were drug addicts.

As you can imagine, this made the rest of my time at school extremely difficult. It was all very embarrassing for my parents too, as other children's parents would call them up and tell them to make sure I stayed well away from their kids. Even at the horse stables, a place that I had always considered a safe haven, was now a place where judgmental stares and rumors followed me. I felt completely alienated, and the whole experience has cast a long shadow of anxiety over my perception of drugs and society to this day.

When Trust Goes Wrong

A few months later I found myself getting entangled with an older individual whom we'll refer to as Jack. I was 15 at the time, Jack around 20. In a small town like ours, everyone knows each other, so it was inevitable that we would meet through mutual acquaintances. Looking back on it now, maybe I thought that it was cool and exciting to hang out with someone more mature and older than me. Despite the age disparity, Jack did initially provide me with a sense of security, a refuge from the tumultuous experiences of adolescence.

Although it appeared harmless at first, an invitation to his place took a sinister turn when suddenly, right in the middle of our conversation, he jumped on top of me and began to feel me inappropriately. I asked him, "What are you doing? What's going on?". He simply replied, "Relax, don't worry" before talking about wanting to have sex with me and beginning to remove my clothes, in spite of my repeated refusals. I started screaming and fighting back but he covered my mouth and held me down, telling me to be quiet because the neighbors might hear. So, I simply accepted my fate.

Following the assault, he drove me home and acted like nothing out of the ordinary had even happened. In the following weeks I experienced feelings of intense shame and even blamed myself for having trusted him and gone to his house in the first place. I was so confused, I don't think I even really looked at it as rape at the time.

Jack's toxic influence only grew after that initial incident. He took advantage of my weaknesses and used my humiliation against me, making me believe I couldn't involve my parents. He continuously attempted to manipulate me, fabricating falsehoods in order to deceive my friends and family, and even making threats to destroy my life if I ended our relationship. It was an absolute nightmare, and I felt trapped.

His manipulation affected not only my friendships, but also my home life. He'd casually drop by for coffee with my unsuspecting parents, making it seem like he was just a friendly acquaintance. However, in private, he would quietly speak toxic words to me, causing me to question my own self-worth. I was stuck in a cycle of fear and self-doubt, unsure of how to escape. When I finally found the courage to confide in my mom, she listened to me with all the compassion and understanding I'd come to rely on. She helped me see that I wasn't alone, and that Jack's manipulation wasn't my fault. The whole experience really has had a profound and lasting impact on me.

When I confided to a friend about Jack, he took it upon himself to play devil's advocate and confront him. Once Jack realized that the cat was finally out of the bag, he eventually left me alone. However, much to my surprise, my friend ended up believing Jack's version of events and formed a friendship with him! Talk about a stab in the back.

Feeling hurt and betrayed, I decided along with one of my girlfriends to somewhat "redecorate" my former friend's apartment. A pretty foolish and naive idea, I know. His neighbors caught us in the act, but we managed to escape because for some reason the police thought they were searching for two adult women in their twenties. Crisis averted!

Fast-forward years later and my friend finally saw the light about Jack, and he apologized for not believing me at the time. It appeared that Jack had developed a taste for sexual assault and had done the exact same thing to someone else! I forgave my friend, and confessed to the apartment redecoration incident. We remain close friends to this day.

A Dance with Panic and Anxiety

I went through some pretty tough stuff with Jack, and it really messed me up. I tried to act like everything was fine, but deep down I was a mess. I would randomly breakdown and cry uncontrollably because I didn't know how to deal with my emotions. My parents noticed something was off and arranged for me to go to therapy. Honestly, those sessions are all a bit of a blur—I can barely remember them. I was eventually diagnosed with a form of PTSD. It was a label that tried to encompass everything that was happening to me, but it still doesn't feel like it fully captures it. Trauma has a strange way of making you doubt everything, including the diagnosis. That's where I found myself—still in the process of figuring things out and healing.

In order to get away from all the rumours and suspicious faces from back home, I enrolled in a school a couple of hours away from my hometown. The new school year brought with it a fresh sense of optimism and a feeling of starting anew, but my past experiences still lingered in the shadows. Still, I was eager for some independence and embraced it by sharing an apartment with like-minded young roommates who were also figuring out their own paths. My life back then was full of ups and downs, but I'll never forget one particular night when things turned sour once again.

One night, following an enjoyable evening spent in the company of friends, I found myself having to walk back home alone. I knew one of my cousin's friends lived in the area, so I thought that I'd stop by and ask to borrow a flashlight from him. Little did I know, that seemingly harmless notion would lead to a night I'd much rather forget.

As I walked into the apartment to collect the flashlight, I was invited to sit and have a beer. The place was full of people and some were passing a joint around. Although I did have some reservations due to my past experience, I decided to take a few puffs anyway. I recall beginning to feel a weird sensation, as if the paintings on the wall were animated and all the sounds around me were warping into one. It dawned on me that the company I was in were all heavy drug users, and the weed they shared was most likely laced with something more potent.

Panic set in, and I became convinced that I was in grave and imminent danger. Desperate for an escape, I searched for a way out of the room. Fortunately, one of the other guests had already contacted a friend for a ride home, so I took the opportunity to hijack her lift to safety.

Not long after we set off however, I felt a panic attack coming on and was struggling to breathe, so I begged him to pull over before jumping out of his car and sprinting towards the closest house. The second the door was opened I rushed past the surprised old man standing there and made my way to the kitchen for some water. After drinking my fill of water, I turned to find an older couple staring at me in total shock.

The rest of the night is all a bit hazy, but the couple managed to get in touch with my mother, who was asleep back home. My roommate eventually picked me up and took me to the hospital, where they diagnosed me with having suffered a severe drug-induced panic attack. After a few hours of tests and treatment, I was released, shaken but very much relieved that it was all over.

The following week, things took another turn for the worse. A simple trip to Ikea with my mom became the trigger for a full-blown panic attack. I was overwhelmed by the busy crowds, all the bright lights, and the seemingly endless rows of identical-looking furniture. My heart felt like it was going to burst straight out of my chest, my mind raced and my body trembled. I felt like I was wrapped in cellophane, suffocating under the weight of my own fear. I was convinced that something sinister had been done to me that night at the apartment.

That was just the beginning however. For six months, I was tormented by panic attacks that left me gasping for air, my mind reeling with dread, and my body exhausted from the constant adrenaline surges. I felt like I was walking on eggshells every day, just waiting for the next attack to strike. My room became both a refuge and a prison, a place where I hid from the world, too afraid to face the world outside.

The anxiety consumed me, turning me into a shadow of my former self. I felt like I was drowning in a sea of fear, unable to escape the darkness that had taken over my life. I was having a hard time processing it all myself, so explaining it to my parents felt futile. I kept it all locked away inside. Trying to get any help from the authorities was a total maze, and Norway's mental health system moved very slowly. By the time someone finally reached out, I had already been fighting this battle on my own for months. I'd gotten so used to dealing with it that therapy now felt unnecessary.

Mallorca: The Oasis of Escapism

The frequent and overwhelming panic attacks obviously had a significant impact on my performance at my new school. In search of yet another fresh start, I decided to move back home with my parents and finish my secondary education in my hometown.

During the next three years, I navigated a tricky relationship and continued to struggle to find my purpose in life. I felt restless, and yearned for a new adventure that would take me beyond my small Norwegian town. One day, a Facebook advertisement caught my eye: Bartending school in Spain! I'd always been drawn to Spain's warmth and culture. I decided to go for it.

Once I had applied and been accepted, the choice lay between Barcelona and the island of Mallorca. As someone who had never been drawn to big city life, the island lifestyle resonated deeply with me. Mallorca—an island paradise nestled in the heart of the Mediterranean—captivated my imagination. Despite my social anxiety and limited language skills (I barely spoke English and spoke zero Spanish), I was determined to push on despite my reservations. The program included room and board but no wages, so using my savings and some financial help from my parents, I was ready to take the leap and embrace the unknown.

I ended up in Magaluf, a town known for its wild party scene and a haven for those who don't quite fit in. I was drawn to its carefree vibe. However, it soon became apparent to me that some people came to Magaluf not just for the party, but to also escape something in their past. There were rumors of fugitives, crooks and runaways blending in with the crowd, also seeking a new start. I didn't ask questions.

Bartending school began in the spring of 2017, and amidst all the chaos of endless foam parties and beach discos, I found a sense of belonging amongst people who came from all walks of life. I soon made a lot of new friends and connections. For a while, alcohol became a convenient therapy for any social anxiety and to block out my past. But as the months went by, the days of beers for breakfast and hostel stays were coming to an end. I had run out of money and realized that I needed to head back home to Norway.

After seven months saving up back in Norway, the allure of the Spanish shores once again pulled me back to Mallorca. With a bartending degree in my back pocket, I decided to embark on another adventure. This time, I had organized a job at a local Norwegian bar in Magaluf which had the added benefit of an apartment which I shared with my co-worker.

In the midst of the wild Magaluf party scene, I met Steven, a guy who stood out from the crowd. He was a successful businessman, living a pretty normal lifestyle despite all the chaos around him. Once the summer season was over, he invited me on a trip far beyond all our usual hangouts in Mallorca to Cape Verde Africa. I made it clear to him that we were only travelling as friends and that I did not have any romantic interest in him at all. He politely agreed and stated that he simply wanted to give me the experience of a lifetime, nothing more. I should've been more cautious, but I was so excited about the opportunity to experience a new country. Little did I know how much of a mistake it would turn out to be at the time.

The Narcissist: A Roundtrip to Hell

The journey to Cape Verde, a place full of promise and adventure, became an absolute nightmare for me that I will never forget. As we were flying in over the beautiful island of Boa Vista, I felt true excitement. I had never been to a place like this before, a tropical island. But even before we checked into the hotel, his demeanour had changed and he started to give off a weird vibe.

A minor issue with the Wi-Fi password got completely blown out of proportion. The hotel required us to create our own password for the Wi-Fi, so I did. However, without realizing it, I had accidently set the password for our whole room, not just my phone. To my dismay, he accused me of trying to hide the password from him for some reason. No matter how hard I tried to explain that it was an honest mistake, he wouldn't listen. Later that night whilst we were eating dinner he brought it up again and began yelling at me in the the restaurant in front of everyone. I couldn't believe it! I was so shocked and embarrassed , I simply tried to ignore him. All of a sudden this Mr. Nice guy was quickly turning into Mr. Ice guy.

Looking back now I think that for some reason Steven had purposefully decided to make my life hell that holiday. Why? I don't know. Maybe he felt empowered by the fact that he was paying for everything and that he therefore had the right to treat me badly. Maybe he was frustrated because he realized he wasn't going to sleep with me. Whatever it was, he did a total 180-degree turn on me. Why do people do the things they do? I still find it hard to believe. I had never experienced such a switch in a character so fast. And there I was, stranded on a tropical island in the middle of the Atlantic with nowhere to go! I began to regret my decision to go on this trip almost immediately, and I'm sorry to say that the torment only got worse from then on.

His jealousy was smothering at times. If I asked the waiter a question about the food and was friendly to him, Steven would accuse me of flirting. I wasn't, but what if I was? We weren't "together" in that way. If I simply looked another man in the eyes that was passing by and smiled, he'd go bananas. If I dressed up in a way that he didn't approve of he'd berate me and call me a whore. Even if I simply looked at my phone quickly, all hell would break loose and he'd accuse me of spending all my time on social media.

Every time I stayed and tried to reason with him, none of my words mattered. If I ran away from the situation, he would follow me and turn that into a brand new argument. He tried so hard to convince me of his truth. Every little thing I did was twisted into proof of his delusions. I tried my best to ignore his fantasies and lies, but in the end all I could do was to focus instead on trying to enjoy the beautiful resort. It was difficult.

I woke up still reeling from the argument the night before but we had already arranged a quad bike tour of the island. We met the group and drove into the desert—it was beautiful. We actually had a good time, enjoying the speed and action. We explored Cape Verde's many sand dunes, caves, and amazing beaches.

At every stop on the trip, we met up with another group travelling from a different hotel. I noticed this one guy from the other group kept looking at me and I kept getting the feeling that I had seen him somewhere before. It was such a strange feeling since we were in the middle of nowhere on a small island, so I didn't think much more of it. That is, until we got back to the resort and I checked my Instagram and saw I had received a message from the guy.

This was very random and quite unbelievable, since the message was from the day before and he had no way of knowing that I was going on that tour. What a huge coincidence! Maybe this random guy had seen a story I had posted on Instagram where I tagged the resort we were staying at, so he decided to message me. I found this all a little bit amusing and decided to tell Steven about it while having dinner at the resort. A big mistake! This random message from a stranger on Instagram turned into a wild accusation of secret meetings and plans to run away together—totally ridiculous, but Steven wouldn't believe me. Or at least he did all he could to make his truth the only truth.

Evenings were torturous as he continued to verbally attack me, calling me names and tearing me down. I think it was on day eight of the trip when we actually got into a physical altercation. After hours of him talking about how horrible I was while laughing in my face, I snapped and went for him, punching him in the chest. He'd finally got his reaction.

There were nights when I'd attempt to go to sleep and he wouldn't allow it. He just wanted to keep arguing, saying things like "you are the worst person I have ever met," and "no one really likes you." I'd lock myself in the bathroom crying and he'd come after me. I'd try leaving the room and he'd follow me, constantly criticizing me and pursuing an argument. I'd go out to our private pool and he'd stand over me whilst insulting me and attacking my self-esteem. It was a total nightmare. I knew that he was trying to push me to a point where I would lose control. In his head this would back up his accusations of me being a psycho, which he kept calling me.

When I think back on it today, I still wonder where he got all the energy to do the things he did, it was his holiday too! It was almost like he enjoyed it. He seemed to be a man with a need to dominate and control. It was easy for me to see that his goal was to mentally break me down, but the motivation behind his behavior? I am not sure.

According to experts, narcissists have a desire to control others because they have a deep-seated need for power, validation, and admiration. They often have a fragile sense of self-worth and use control over others as a way to feel important, superior, and in charge. By controlling vulnerable people, they can manipulate them into providing the attention, praise, and obedience that they crave. Additionally, control allows them to maintain a sense of predictability and stability. Ultimately, the need for control is a symptom of their underlying emotional issues and insecurities. I'm no expert but I had suddenly found myself isolated on a small island with a guy that I believed to definitely fit that description.

After two weeks of all the abuse our time in Cape Verde was finally over. I flew back to Norway and we went our separate ways. That two-week winter get-away was a living hell and the emotional scars would take a long time to heal. The experience left me shaken and very much aware of how dangerous narcissistic behavior can be.

CHAPTER 3
A Friend Across the Street

Let me introduce you to Rick, a British guy who is a couple of years older than me. It was in September 2018 that I initially crossed paths with him, three months prior to my Cape Verde trip. He worked at a bar across the street from where I was employed. Our first encounters were the usual casual greetings between people that work next to each other. He handled the terrace setup for his bar, while I managed my responsibilities at the bar where I worked.

Over time, our interactions became more meaningful, progressing from all the usual small talk to authentic discussions about our daily lives. He confessed to me his growing fatigue of the bar scene in Magaluf, which I could relate to due to my own increasing discomfort with the way alcohol was impacting my health. Our connection grew over a few weeks, but my departure to Norway temporarily put a pause on our friendship.

During my winter visit to Norway, I reflected on the toll alcohol had taken on my physical and mental well-being. Determined to embrace a healthier lifestyle in the future, I decided I would try to maintain a healthy daily routine when I eventually returned to Magaluf. In March of the following year, I met up with Rick again. Although it was still the winter season, which meant fewer job opportunities, this afforded us the chance to explore more of what the island had to offer.

Our shared desire for a life free from excessive drinking brought us closer together. Nevertheless, it's important to highlight that we were just good friends at this point. There was no inkling of romantic involvement; rather, he emerged as a new and supportive friend.

As our friendship deepened, I discovered that we shared similar perspectives on life and a desire for a different future. Our bond grew into something profound, and he provided me with a valuable confidant who truly understood and accepted me.

We attempted to adopt healthier lifestyles by reducing our alcohol intake and engaging in activities like running. However, the stress of our jobs, especially my role in a busy bar, led to more drinking as a coping mechanism. It was a constant battle.

Despite some red flags and potential signs that our friendship might be evolving into something more for Rick, I chose to overlook them, convinced that he valued our friendship just as much as I did. There was also a lingering fear of possibly losing his friendship, which clouded my judgment. I acknowledged the possibility that he might desire more, but he consistently reassured me of his commitment to maintaining our platonic bond.

Three months later, I decided to move in with Rick and a female friend of his in order to save some money. Side note: ever heard of a roommate from hell? Well, that was her. Dirty clothes everywhere including under the kitchen table which doubled as her closet. Spoiled food and dirty dishes as far as the eye can see. Cat urine spread about everywhere. Homeless drug addicts popping by for extended stays. Anyway, despite having some doubts about his true intentions, Rick kept showing me that he was still committed to our friendship. Even when we shared a bedroom, he was respectful of boundaries, which made me feel comfortable.

Things took a turn however, when my cousin and best friend Ylva came to visit me from Norway. She and I had decided to book a hotel room without him. That was the first time I ever saw a different side of Rick. One evening, at the restaurant where we were eating, he suddenly showed up out of nowhere and became extremely jealous that I was spending time with my cousin and not him. He said that we were going out partying and having fun without him. He started accusing me of things in front of everyone saying that I was a whore and I was sleeping around even though I wasn't. To make things worse, he was obviously drunk and messed up. Again, in spite of my suspicions, I didn't want to make a big deal of it at the time so I simply brushed it aside. Looking back, it's clear that our friendship was beginning to get complicated.

Return to the homeland

Rick and I had been talking about making changes for a while that summer. The non-stop drinking and partying had really taken its toll, and I was worried about where it might all lead. I let him know that I had made the decision to return to Norway. I expressed to him the importance of going back to Norway for my overall well-being. There was never any intention on my part to actively try to persuade him to accompany me, although it would have been nice to have him come, since he had become such a close friend. In the end, I departed in late July while he remained in Magaluf to sort things out.

After I had been in Norway for a few weeks, he started asking me about possible job opportunities. I wanted to help him in any way that I could because he was like a brother to me, even though I hadn't found a job yet myself, and I was undecided about exactly which city in Norway I wanted to move to. As a result, we talked things over and decided that he would fly over and we'd explore the country—which was new to him—and look for potential opportunities whilst doing so.

Rick arrived at my parents' place in the summer of 2019, and for the first couple of weeks, we enjoyed each other's company, heading out to my parents' cabin in the woods, indulging in fishing, and relishing the camaraderie. During this period, he still embodied the same cheerful friend I had met in Magaluf, and everything seemed to be going fine. We made the decision to depart on our road trip after those first weeks. We aimed to have a once-in-a-lifetime kind of experience, visiting Norway's fjords, her majestic mountains, lush greenery and to also search for job opportunities in all the different regions we visited along the way.

One of our stops was Drammen, a city that held a special place in my heart as I had lived there a few years prior. Located just 30 minutes outside of Oslo, Drammen was one of my top choices for settling down due to its unique charm. The Drammenselva River runs through the city center, which adds to its scenic beauty. Additionally, Drammen has a lively social scene with plenty of cultural events and a great selection of restaurants and cafes.

We spent our nights sleeping in the car, a big Mercedes station wagon with mattresses in the back, making hotel reservations unnecessary. This unconventional mode of travel and sleeping arrangements allowed us to experience the country in a practical and adventurous way. While in Drammen, I submitted job applications and assisted Rick in looking for suitable opportunities, taking into account the additional challenges he faced as a foreigner from England needing a work permit.

While waiting for responses from prospective employers, we continued our road trip, exploring Norway's stunning south coast and eventually reaching the charming city of Stavanger on the west coast. Our first priority was finding a suitable spot to park the car for the night. We strolled through the historic cobblestone streets, admiring the unique colorful wooden houses, and made our way to the picturesque harbor. The sun was shining, and I felt a serene sense of contentment, secure in the knowledge that I had made the right decision to move back to Norway.

One evening, we decided to reconnect with some friends I had met in Magaluf years before. The night started off well, but an unexpected disagreement arose when I got caught up in a long conversation with my old friend from Stavanger, leaving Rick feeling neglected. Impulsively, he took the car keys and left, leaving me annoyed and perplexed. I chose to avoid further drama however and spent the night with my friend. The next day, he apologized and admitted that he had overreacted. We agreed to forget about the whole episode and move forward, even though I did have some reservations.

Not long after, I received a message from a potential employer in Drammen so I eagerly scheduled an interview for the next day. Excited about this new opportunity, we rushed back in order to make it in time. I ended up getting a sales job at the company. Suddenly I found myself starting a new career in an exciting new city but with no apartment, and only a car to sleep in. Wanting to get settled as best I could before going to work, I reached out to an old friend who managed the school in Drammen where I had previously studied. Thankfully, he provided us with a room as a temporary solution until Rick and I could find our own apartment.

Our apartment search proved challenging as we had to balance the cost of an apartment along with all our preferences and the need for two bedrooms. Eventually, we encountered a newly renovated apartment with two bedrooms that captured my heart. It was centrally located, not too large or small and with excellent amenities. It was with great excitement and anticipation that we decided to make it our home.

Difficulties soon arose however, as Rick had to go through a bureaucratic nightmare due to the work permit process taking at least a month of navigating through different offices and requirements. Despite the difficulties, my mother graciously assisted in paying for his portion of the deposit, and he obtained a loan from my mother and his uncle in Canada to handle the initial expenses. Eventually, he got his job, and I continued working mine, leading to a relatively peaceful period. We settled into our routines, yet little did I suspect that unforeseen challenges were lurking just around the corner.

I found myself grappling with some very unsettling incidents in our friendship that raised some serious concerns about its true nature. Despite not sensing any romantic interest from him, there was a palpable sense of obligation, as if I had to be constantly by his side to prevent him from becoming miserable when left alone. This feeling intensified whenever I went out with other groups of friends. He would unexpectedly show up out of the blue and launch into a barrage of baseless accusations similar to the disturbing episode in Magaluf when my cousin was present. He would try to cause emotional distress, by labelling me as a slob, a whore, and a bad person in general.

Despite these pretty alarming warning signs, I chose to downplay them, particularly since we were sharing an apartment. As time passed, I consciously distanced myself from him and focused instead on my job, friendships, and the demands of working long hours. However, it soon became apparent that he was discontent, leading to some pretty uncomfortable situations. One such incident occurred when I was taking a shower. I suddenly sensed an eerie presence outside my bathroom door, which had a key-hole near the handle that someone could peer through if they wanted to. I got out of the shower and flung the door open. Rick jumped back, startled, and flew across the room in a panic. I confronted him about watching me but of course he stubbornly denied everything.

Christmas time was now soon approaching and I had to decide how to handle the holidays. I confided in my mom about my reservations regarding Rick's behavior. After talking it over with her, we came to the conclusion that maybe I was being a bit paranoid. So, despite my concerns I invited Rick to spend the holidays with my family, since he had no plans to spend the holidays with his family in England. Earlier that year I had travelled to England with him for his friend's wedding and got to meet his family. They seemed like such lovely people, so I found it very peculiar that he wouldn't want to spend the holidays at home with them.

The holiday season back home seemed harmonious at first, and Rick's relationship with my parents blossomed. However, signs of his clinginess resurfaced during an outing, which began to create an uncomfortable atmosphere. Tensions escalated when I went out with friends, leaving him at home and visibly bothered. Later that night, I returned home with a male friend. In a gesture of good will, I had offered to let him stay at my parents' house, in a separate bedroom, since he lived so far away. This very obviously bothered Rick and by the next morning something had changed, he was acting different, quiet and distant. Although we weren't scheduled to travel back to Drammen for another few days, he was on a train back later that very same morning.

In early January, when I returned home to our apartment, I was shocked to see that Rick had dismantled our Christmas tree and taken down all the festive decorations, despite our prior agreement to keep them up for a while. He was very aware of how much Christmas meant to me. It has always been my absolute favorite time of the year. He knew how much I loved coming home and being surrounded by everything Christmas-related. His actions felt like a deliberate slight, although he insisted that he was doing me a favor by putting the decorations away for me. Still, I couldn't shake off the feeling that something was amiss and by mid-January I was sensing a palpable shift in our friendship that made me feel increasingly uneasy. It was then that I began to make a deliberate effort to keep my distance.

Bali

As January drew to a close, I was thrilled to embark on a working vacation to Bali with some of my colleagues. It was my first time visiting the island and to my surprise, Rick was extremely helpful and supportive, seemingly showing genuine enthusiasm for my adventure. The day I was due to leave, he stayed up to assist me with all my luggage and even walked me to the train station in the middle of the night.

Twenty-four hours later, and I had arrived in paradise! Our group of eight young friends checked into a stunning beachfront villa, steps away from one of the island's best beach clubs. We dove straight into the tropical bliss, indulging in exotic drinks, savoring delicious food, and basking under the warm sun of the Indian ocean. Laughter and joy followed us everywhere we went. I even tried surfing for the first time, enjoyed corn on the cob from a street vendor, and marvelled at the breathtaking sunset whilst sat on a scooter. It was pure paradise, and I was truly in my happy place.

One evening, we decided to go out bar hopping, and I found myself in a troubling situation that left me shaken. During a visit to one of Bali's many clubs, I met a guy from Russia. We were enjoying each other's company, chatting away and having a good time, but I began to feel tired and wasn't really feeling the club scene so I decided to call it a night. He accompanied me outside in order to search for a taxi, but then offered to take me home on his scooter instead. In my tired state, and having had a fair few drinks, I naively agreed.

I soon noticed however, that we weren't heading in the right direction, but he kept assuring me that we were just going to make a quick stop at his place because he wanted to show me the beautiful view. After telling him no several times, I started to worry and get upset, but he continued to insist. I tried to stay calm but inside I was panicking. Where was this night going to end? Had I made a terrible decision? There wasn't much I could do to derail his plans so I decided to go with the flow and try not to make things worse. Thirty minutes later we arrived at his place. I remember him serving me a drink but the rest of the details of that night are very hazy. There are memories of my head in the toilet and of me waking up early the next morning, desperate to get home. In a panic, I tried to rush out of his apartment but after realizing I was in the middle of nowhere, I took him up on his offer to give me a ride back to my villa.

After a few hours of thinking the nights events over, I consciously decided to put it all behind me and continue to enjoy my Bali adventure as best I could, grateful to be okay and unharmed. Lesson learned? Don't jump on a scooter with a random guy in the middle of nowhere in a strange, distant foreign land.

As the holiday went on, I felt the need to call Rick and share my unsettling experience, hoping he would provide some level of support. However, far from being supportive, his response was alarming and accusatory, labeling me as a "horrible person" who "deserved it." He hurled dehumanizing insults at me, telling me to "go kill myself" and that I was "a worthless whore." He sounded like an unhinged madman. It's hard for me to remember everything he said that day but it was some of the worst things you can ever say to a person. He used degrading and humiliating words to belittle and diminish me. This incident really marked another huge warning sign in our relationship, and should have revealed to me that our friendship was no longer sustainable. When I returned from Bali I confronted Rick about his reaction on the phone, making it clear that our relationship dynamic needed to change. As we still had six months left on the contract, we could still share the apartment, but I told him we needed to lead separate lives as I simply couldn't tolerate being spoken to like that and I didn't appreciate his drama.

CHAPTER 4
The Nightmare Descends

Being Watched

Over the next few weeks, I kept feeling a disturbing sense of being watched whilst taking a shower. For my own peace of mind, I resorted to placing paper over that small hole in the bathroom door, ensuring that he couldn't intrude on my privacy. He kept asking me about it, and I would offer a vague explanation that it made me feel more comfortable. On occasion however, there were instances when I'd find the paper removed.

The unsettling behavior escalated when Rick began to leave handwritten notes for me around the apartment. Every day I'd discover notes placed in odd locations, saying things like "You're a queen," "You rock my world," and other complimentary messages. These notes seemed to appear everywhere—in my bedroom, on the toilet seat, and even beside me on my bed when I woke up in the morning. Was he watching me as I slept?

Although the feeling of being watched persisted, I initially dismissed it as perhaps childish immature behavior on his part. Additionally, his tendency to show up unexpectedly when I was out with other people started to become more and more frequent and I felt he was encroaching on my personal space.

Some of Rick's acquaintances began to reach out to me. I started receiving disturbing messages from some of Rick's colleagues, expressing concern for his physical and psychological well-being. They had been made aware by some people close to Rick that he would sometimes spend entire days confined to his bedroom. This prompted genuine concern for his mental state. Other messages referred to his issues with alcohol, as a lot of his colleagues had noticed he frequently smelled of alcohol at work, which lead to the loss of both of his jobs—one due to his alcohol-scented presence and the other because of absenteeism and intoxication.

Around the end of February, a significant turning point occurred. Rick's job troubles and strange behavior made it clear that living together was no longer sustainable for me.

Less Money, More Problems

Due to Rick losing both of his jobs, financial strain inevitably ensued. He struggled to contribute his share of the rent and other living expenses, meaning that I had to assume these responsibilities entirely. What was even more frustrating was the fact that whilst trying to discuss these financial challenges with him, I encountered a side of him that seemed completely detached from reality. He displayed a lack of comprehension about how the world works, repeatedly assuring me that everything would work out fine. This financial burden resulted in me having to repeatedly tap into my savings in order to cover his share of expenses.

Looking back on it now, I ask myself if this was a deliberate move on his part. Was he consciously trying to orchestrate a situation that would unfold in a way that would somehow benefit him whilst putting extra strain on me?

As time went on, I worked while he constantly stayed in his room, failing to address his growing problems. This created even more stress for me, causing me a lot of anger and frustration. I felt resentful towards him and the difficult situation he had put me in. I suspected he was struggling with depression, as he barely ate and had lost so much weight. Even though I would consistently invite him to join me for dinner, my emotions were always mixed - I was both concerned for him and yet annoyed that he was doing so little to improve his own circumstances.

At the beginning of all the confusion and chaos surrounding the COVID-19 pandemic, I continued going to work until my employer decided to send us all home due to the escalating situation. Fortunately, my role allowed me to transition smoothly in to remote work, and I could engage in online tasks and handle emails from home effectively. However, a month after the pandemic took hold, I decided to resign due to the fact that they had changed my hours and made some unauthorized alterations to my compensation plan that I wasn't happy with. So, I decided to go into business for myself with inCruises, an online travel membership club, and Rick decided to start working with me too.

This unexpected shift seemed to elicit genuine joy and optimism from Rick, as he saw it as an opportunity for us to spend more time together. In his mind, with gyms, bars, and restaurants shutting down, the lockdown created the perfect scenario in which our companionship could rekindle. With the absence of external distractions, I was open to the possibility that this could indeed be a good time to try to reconnect with the friend that I once knew, the one capable of bringing humor and enjoyment into my life. Besides, did I really have a choice? My goal was really just to make the best out of a bad situation since the pandemic left me with no other option, plus we had several months left on our lease. During this time, our friendship experienced a kind of resurgence as we found ourselves engaged in various activities such as hiking and movie nights, making the most of the enforced shared time at home.

Snapchat Hacked

The ominous atmosphere soon returned however, when one tumultuous night, my sleep was abruptly shattered when Rick burst into my bedroom, and urgently informed me that my phone and Snapchat had fallen victim to a malicious hack. He had been told by my cousin Ylva, who had been unable to reach me directly. The intruder had not only gained access to my private content but had shamelessly exposed pictures and videos of me, capturing carefree moments with my cousin from the previous summer in Magaluf. Bewildered, I rushed to check my Snapchat, which confirmed the compromising nature of the leaked content.

I swiftly deleted all the leaked material and convinced myself that I had successfully mitigated the situation. Despite numerous messages from friends and family expressing concern, I dismissed the incident as a one-off isolated event. I failed to grasp the gravity of the situation as a whole and in my naivety, I overlooked the potential long-term consequences of having my privacy violated in this way.

The following week brought an unexpected connection with a random Instagram user from Arizona. Amidst the chaos of the pandemic, communicating with someone so far removed from my immediate reality provided a strange sense of comfort. The back-and-forth conversations went on for about a month. We talked about family, potential business ventures and the happenings of our day-to-day lives.

Paul came across as a friendly, understanding and interesting human being. After a while he made me feel like I could open up to him and I told him about my issues with Rick. At one point I even mentioned to him that I thought I might be living with a psychopath.

Our interactions quickly turned unsettling however, when Paul suggested he would pay me for compromising photographs of myself, an offer I strongly refused. After he apologized to me, I decided to try and move past it; but it did change my opinion of him, and I proceeded with far more caution.

Not soon after, I found out that my grandmother was sick and close to dying. I had always been very close to her so it upset me quite a lot that my family and I were unable to see her at first due to COVID restrictions. We were eventually allowed to see her shortly before her death, but it was still such a sad and depressing time for me.

Rick decided that he wanted to do something nice for me to try to help me feel better, so he decided to accompany me on my trip to Oslo. Whilst it was a nice gesture, I kept wondering how he was able to afford to do all this while struggling to pay his share of the rent. He confessed to me that he had sold nude pictures of himself online for money and that he would cover the rent when we returned. Okay...WOW!

The following day, whilst I was having lunch with Rick in Oslo, I received a message from Paul stating that he was very serious about his initial offer, so much so that he said he was on his way to the bank to transfer $50,000 as proof that he was for real. He even sent me a photo showing someone who I presumed to be him, entering a bank.

I decided to confide this whole crazy story to Rick, and we decided to go along for the ride and test Paul a bit. The messaging back and forth went on for days but then suddenly the situation escalated when Paul began sending me all the content from my leaked and hacked Snapchat account. I was shocked and in a panic. I began questioning who this guy was. What did he want? How did he get those pictures? I told Rick what was going on and he was also shocked and concerned. Rick and I both agreed that it would be best if we simply ignored Paul from now on and just let it go. That turned out to be a lot harder than we anticipated.

Not long after I began ignoring him, Paul started to send me compromising pictures that only I had access to on my phone. He must have somehow known that money was tight as he offered to pay me a lot of money. He also threatened to expose these pictures to all my family and friends unless I complied with more explicit photo demands. It felt like my whole world was beginning to fall apart. I had so many questions! How did he hack my phone? What was his end game? Why was he doing this to me?

In a desperate move to make it all go away and burdened by economic pressures, I said to myself, "Heck, if this guy is stupid enough to send me money and I can make this all go away, I'll do it!" So, I reluctantly decided to send him one more compromising picture in the hope of ending the entire ordeal. However, this act only seemed to intensify his demands. Overwhelmed and desperate, I turned to drinking as a coping mechanism in order to deal with the mounting stress and uncertainty of the situation I had found myself in. But Paul was relentless and he wanted more and more, whilst all the while assuring me that if I sent him just one last picture, it would all end. So, I did.

The torment would persist however, and Paul's demands became increasingly explicit and degrading. The initial persona I had opened myself up to in our initial communications was gone. His tone had turned sadistic. He would say things like "you don't know what I'm capable of. I can end you. I can end your life. I can turn your life upside down with the snap of my fingers." He was really getting into my head. Under my skin. He began to not only threaten me but my family as well. He made me feel like I would be in real life threatening danger if I didn't follow his every instruction to the letter. He would constantly refer to himself as "they" and "we" leading me to believe that there were others involved which led me to freak out even more.

The frequency and tone of the messages started to become overwhelming. They came in at all hours of the day and night. Torturing me psychologically. Making me question my safety and my sanity. The explicit content initially hacked from my phone, plus the pictures I had sent him, further intensified my sense of anguish and vulnerability.

Not only did Paul bring up details about my family that only someone close to me could ever know, which made it all the more difficult for me to comprehend, but now he started to bring up Rick as well. By late summer, Rick had also started to receive messages from Paul, and he showed me messages going back about a week. He claimed that he hadn't initially shared the messages with me because he didn't want to worry me. Rick was freaking out too. He was scared.

Paul stated that he was happy to finally have both of our attention. He kept reminding us that if we didn't comply with his requests that my family was in danger and that the whole world would see all the compromising picture's he had of me. He claimed to be a very powerful man, with many people at his disposal who were willing and able to do his bidding in order to go through with his threats. I became paranoid and felt like I was being watched at every turn.

This next part is going to shock you. The psychological manipulation and intimidation reached a point where Paul began to demand that Rick and I engage in intimate sexual acts, multiple times, each instance more degrading and humiliating than the last. I won't get into details because it's all too hurtful and unnecessary, but you can use your imagination. They were the types of things you'd only ever do with someone you love and a lot of other things most of us would never even consider doing.

Initially, Rick and I resisted Paul's demands. We simply said, "Not gonna happen." I want you to understand something. I viewed Rick like a brother. And I've already described to you everything we had been through. I had zero interest in Rick romantically or sexually. He was fighting through this nightmare alongside me. When Paul first asked for these performances, he stated that if we didn't comply there would be massive repercussions. He asked for screenshots as visual proof that we had done what had been asked of us. Rick and I tried to figure out ways to fake it - but it never worked. We had no choice but to do what was asked of us. It totally broke me. I felt disgusted, used and humiliated. These acts were coerced under the constant threat of Paul exposing all the compromising and intrusive videos to my family as well as the constant threat of violence.

Although we were sending him all the requested screenshots, he had also somehow managed to gain access to the videos we filmed. At this point I hadn't made the connection that he must have been the one responsible for the phone hacking incident that had happened all those months prior. Plus, neither of us were in a particularly good place mentally. In all honesty, we were in the middle of Covid, trapped in an apartment because of the lockdowns, struggling financially, drinking to cope, utterly run down and depressed. I wasn't thinking straight. It was hard to put all the pieces of this diabolical and complex puzzle together. It was the perfect storm. The tormentor held such a tight grip over my life, manipulating my every move and decision. Even the smallest deviation from his instructions carried with it the threat of immediate punishment, either through explicit physical and psychological abuse or by him deleting videos and demanding a repeat performance.

During this period, Rick showed apparent signs of distress and vulnerability, comforting me in the toughest moments. He would say things like, "We can stop if you want. We don't need to keep going but I just want everything to be okay." During this time, I spent most of the day crying my eyes out and he was the only person I could turn to. Rick and I were in this together, he was also receiving messages mirroring those sent to me.

I had become so paranoid and broken by this point, that one day I actually sat down and started to jot down all the names of the people who I thought might possibly be responsible for the ordeal I was going through. Rick's name was on that list because one day I noticed that Paul's writing style reflected the writing style of some of Rick's messages from before. I also realized that Paul sometimes wrote things and used phrases that only Rick and I would use with each other. Paul had told us that he was always listening to us, which made me think that he knew everything that was going on. This caused me to question my theory. Was I simply being paranoid or was I actually on to something? This all further clouded my perception, making it hard for me to tell friend from foe.

The tormentor's demands began to extend far beyond explicit sexual content; he also orchestrated scenarios involving violence and

THE NIGHTMARE DESCENDS

harm. Bizarrely, he instructed me to physically assault Rick and vice versa, creating a disturbing cycle of physical and mental abuse that blurred the lines between reality and the virtual nightmare that I found myself trapped in. Have you ever been punched hard in the face by a man? I had never experienced being punched in the face by anyone in my entire life! Imagine submitting to it willingly and recording it over and over in order to make sure the video shows everything and is acceptable to a faceless blackmailer.

Being punched in the face is bad enough, but for me, knowing it was coming was terrifying. Doing it over and over again to make sure it was bad enough to be accepted by our tormentor was even worse. At least I had the foresight to keep all the videos as proof of my ordeal.

When I was asked to come back in to work for the summer season, my face was all bruised and swollen so I told them that I had been involved in a serious car accident, but would be able to start the following week—we needed the money.

Attempts to resist or question the tormentor's commands were swiftly met with aggressive and often terrifying rebuffs. They had complete control over my phone, regularly deleting any evidence of their demands,

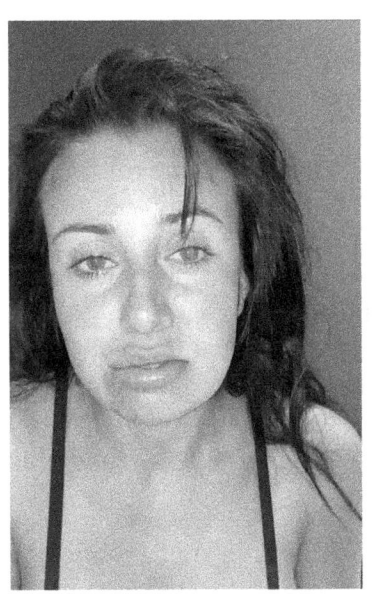

making it almost impossible to prove their manipulation tactics. We would attempt to make a video following his instructions as best we could but the second I went over to my phone to take the screenshot, the video was nowhere to be found. I was in such a paranoid state, I didn't even trust myself anymore—had I forgotten to press record? The psychological toll of this continuous cycle of degradation, violence, and manipulation left me in a perpetual state of fear, anxiety, and despair.

My attempts to seek professional help were stifled at every turn. Any interaction with friends or colleagues could result in a potential threat against their safety. The tormentor monitored my every move and swiftly punished any deviation from his instructions. I would walk past the police station every day on my commute to work and back. I remember regularly sitting down on a bench outside the police station hoping someone would notice me and ask if I needed any help. I was too scared to ever enter the station, and I would receive messages whilst sitting outside, letting me know that if I did reach out to anyone, Paul would end my life. It was absolute torture to me. Every day I came home, sat in front of the kitchen window and just watched the people walking past, wondering if I would ever be able to live a normal life again.

Throughout this harrowing ordeal, the tormentor's messages took on an even more sadistic tone. The requests were getting so obscene and the threats so bad. I felt hopeless and completely trapped. I had totally lost control of myself and was too scared to even think about my family. Paul's knowledge of my every move, my private conversations, and my innermost fears added a complex layer of suspicion to the whole situation, leaving me feeling utterly exposed and defenseless. The first message of the day would arrive the second I woke up, the next while I got dressed; then more messages when I opened the fridge, left for work, and upon my arrival there. I would get sent messages detailing to me exactly what I was doing.

Paul's requests took on an even more malevolent tone when he demanded that I start a romantic relationship with Rick on Facebook. Just like that, his commands went from acts of violence towards each other to being loving and caring towards each other. He had already put me through so much up to this point, but almost all of it had been kept behind the walls of our apartment. This particular demand would take my torment out into the public sphere for the first time. I knew that everyone knew about my friendship with Rick, and I also knew that some people thought that we might of had a romantic relationship. The second we clicked on the button to accept the relationship status update on Facebook I completely broke down. I ran into the bathroom locking the door behind me, before sitting down and crying for the next couple hours. By now I was unable to see a way out, no way to ever be free again.

In spite of this, through the midst of all the turmoil, I never lost the will to carry on. Even though I still grappled with the desperate question of how to escape the clutches of these invisible tormentors, who seemed to hold my life in their malevolent hands, the desire to fight on and get through my predicament never wavered.

My 100% Norwegian

During the summer of 2020, the tones of the messages began to change again. It now seemed like Paul was turning against Rick. He started to say that Rick didn't deserve me, and that this had been made evident by his willingness to shoot videos of him punching me in the face and vice versa. He made me feel like my actions would determine Rick's fate. The message was clear: if we didn't comply with his increasingly crazy and erratic requests, Rick's life was in danger.

Even though I had been through a phase where I strongly suspected Rick to have some sort of involvement in all of this, I felt that I had seen genuine fear in his eyes. Paul started sending me messages saying "MY 100% NORWEGIAN...IT IS ALL SORTED MY 100% NORWEGIAN...YOU ARE MY 100% NORWEGIAN...HE IS NOT GOING TO BE A PROBLEM ANYMORE...WE NEED HIM GONE...." And because I lived with Rick, I shared this daunting and intimidating experience with him. I obviously cared. I feared for both his life and mine.

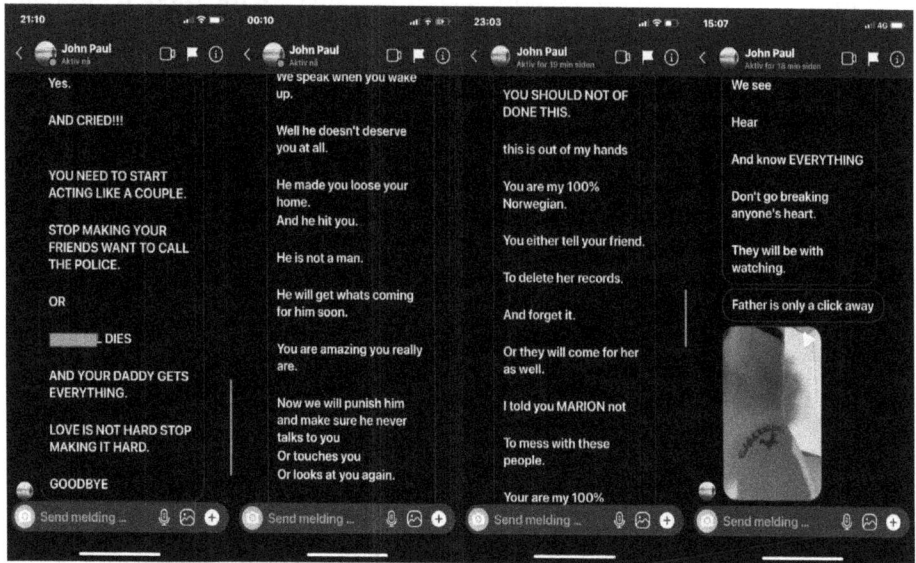

This development stirred something in me and I finally found the courage to act decisively. One day at work, I decided to try something from my work laptop as I knew my tormentor didn't have access to it. I had talked to Rick earlier that day about my intentions to reach out for help and contact the police, but I was taken aback when he totally freaked out on me and said it would put both of us in danger. In spite of this, I had made my decision to go through with my plan.

I found the Facebook page of the police and sent them a message. I knew I had to act quickly; I only sent a short message saying that I was in trouble and described my situation in very few words before asking for help. A couple of minutes later I received a text message from Paul saying that if I didn't tell the police it was all a stupid joke, my family would be hurt that very same evening. I sat there crying contemplating my limited options—but at the end of the day my family always comes first, so I told the police it was just a silly joke.

Their response was both surprising and disheartening: they told me it was a crime to waste police time and that I would get in trouble if I continued to play games with the police force. I had hoped and prayed that they would be perhaps a little bit more pro-active and read between the lines or do some follow-up investigation into my request for help. Not long after I ended the facebook chat I received a message from Paul: "WELL DONE MY 100% NORWEGIAN."

A Glimpse of Hope

In the middle of all the fear, confusion, and desperation to get my life back, I received a message from Anette, one of my oldest and closest friends from my hometown. In the message she said she was worried about me, since no one had heard from me in a couple of weeks. She told me she was on her way to see me to make sure that I was okay. Her social media notification about me entering into a relationship with Rick on Facebook was what made the alarm bells go off for her. The people close to me knew how I felt about him.

The message from her both scared me and gave me a little bit of hope at the same time. I was scared because I knew that someone else had control over my phone and could see whatever messages I received. But I also felt a small glimmer of hope because I knew she wouldn't leave me without being sure that I was okay.

Anette arrived the next day accompanied by another mutual friend called Greg. As I nervously went to the Drammen train station to meet them, I didn't check my phone all morning knowing that reading any messages from Paul would have scared me too much to have even shown up. With my phone in my pocket, I met with my friends, and we decided to go to a local park to hang out.

Immediately, I could sense Anette's concern. I was trying to figure out in my head a way to let her know that I needed help without being explicit which would invoke the wrath of Paul. Once we had all sat down in the park, I whispered in her ear that I couldn't talk openly because "they" were listening. As I shared this information with her my body began shaking with fear and my face started to contort. I will never forget the look on her face. The pity in her eyes broke my heart. She looked at me as if I had completely lost it. She told me that I was in a state of psychosis and needed serious professional help to get better.

After a while of trying to act like it was something we could talk about later, I decided I had to show her. I walked off to some bushes about 50 meters away, threw my phone into them, walked back and said, "now you will see." While my phone was laying in a bush 50 meters away, I told her a shortened version of everything that was going on. She still looked at me as if I was an absolute nutcase. I then told her to get ready for what I knew was coming.

I went over to get my phone, before quickly walking back and opening the messages right in front of her. I had received messages telling me that I had made a bad choice talking to my friend and that consequences were to come. At that point I showed her the entire history of the conversation and she took pictures of it as evidence. Anette finally believed me and saw what I was going through. I had gotten through to someone at last. Still, we decided that this was going to be our day so we bought some drinks and decided we would have fun together like in the old days.

An Evening of Terror

While we were all enjoying ourselves in the park, Rick showed up out of the blue. He joined the party and tried to be part of the group. It all seemed fine. We had our fun at the park before deciding to go back home and make dinner together.

Rick , my two friends from my hometown and I, were all seemingly enjoying each other's company. We spent the afternoon cooking, eating, drinking, and laughing—and for the first time in a long time I was actually having a good time.

Earlier, we had all decided to put our phones away in order to just try and live in the moment. Eventually however we decided that we had to check. As soon as we looked at our phones, we saw that Paul had sent us messages claiming that "they" were in the area and were watching our every move. Greg freaked out and bolted out the door, leaving me, Anette, and Rick at the house. Later on, I found out that whilst I was in the bathroom, Greg had told Anette and Rick that he believed that Rick was the one responsible for everything that was happening.

Soon after, things quickly took on an even more nightmarish turn when Rick began to receive chilling messages instructing him to go outside and "sacrifice" himself for me. We were all unsure as to what "sacrifice" meant—did it mean he would be killed, beaten or kidnapped? It was all so surreal, like a scene straight out of a horror movie. Our tormentors told us that our every move was being monitored, so we began lying on the floor in order to avoid being seen through any of the windows and potentially even getting shot at.

The surreal demand left us in a claustrophobic state of panic and disbelief. Rick, convinced that he needed to comply with the demand in order to protect me, began steeling himself to go outside, ready to face an ominous fate. He was crying uncontrollably. We all were. Bearing witness to my friend's emotional breakdown and facing the prospect of something terrible happening to him shook me to my very core. Desperation set in as we contemplated the unthinkable scenario unfolding before us.

Fearing for our lives, we all decided that we simply had to call the police even though we had been specifically instructed by our tormentors not to do so. While waiting for them to arrive, the panic and desperation intensified. Rick remained determined to go outside and sacrifice himself for me. I tried to stop him by jumping on top of him and held him down as Anette sobbed uncontrollably on the floor right beside us.

The minutes felt like hours as we waited for the police to arrive, and when I finally saw blue lights approach the house, I ran outside in relief. The arrival of law enforcement offered a glimmer of hope, but their response was tepid and dismissive, despite us showing them multiple screenshots as proof of our evening's ordeal. Unbelievably, they actually laughed and seemed reluctant to grasp the severity of the situation.

After trying to explain everything that had led up to this moment, and initially feeling a sense of hope now that law enforcement would be involved—they basically dismissed it all. They spoke to us in Norwegian so that Rick wouldn't understand and attributed all the threats solely to him, without the need for any further thorough investigation. I couldn't believe it. Here they were, basically confirming our fears that Rick was behind it all, and yet they decided to leave us there with the person they felt was responsible for the nightmare I had been living?

The police's lack of intervention and seeming lack of empathy and understanding left us in a state of frustration and despair. The realization that the tormentor might be someone close to me, possibly even Rick, added another layer of horror to an already frightening situation. The rediscovered trust that had recently defined our friendship quickly crumbled, and was replaced with suspicion and fear. All the while Rick kept denying his involvement, claiming that he was also a victim of the situation. The messages continued to persist throughout the evening, but eventually we all decided to go to our rooms, hoping that we would survive the night. Anette went with me to my room and Rick went to his alone.

Morning brought with it a fresh, grim reality. I found Rick sitting on the floor of his room motionless, looking as if he had been sat there the entire night. He had a gaunt, blank stare on his face, like something had changed deep inside him. He was clearly in a state of distress, as if the weight of the accusations had finally broken him. The idea that my roommate might be involved in the torment shattered my sense of security. I didn't want to believe it. How sick would someone have to be to create this elaborate scheme and put not only me but himself through so much, whilst at the same time pretending to be my closest ally and a victim as well? I struggled to make sense of it all. How was he able to pull this off? Who else was involved? How exactly could anyone have done such a thing?

The ordinary act of going to work that morning felt like an intense and perilous journey, fraught with the incessant threats that kept coming in from "Paul."

Throughout work that day, the threats continued. However, the previous night's events with my friends had given me a small sense of power and I became more determined than ever to do something now. I reached out to Bill, one of my closest friends in Drammen, and asked him to swing by where I worked. While I was messaging my friend, Paul went totally mad and wouldn't stop talking about all the danger I was putting myself and others in. But I felt like we had been in so much danger the night before that it was either now or never. Seeking solace, I confided in Bill, sharing with him all of the horrors that had unfolded up to that point. The support of a friend provided me with a temporary respite, a momentary escape from the suffocating grip of my tormentor.

The revelation that Rick, whom I had considered such a close friend, might actually be the source of all this torture left me paralyzed with fear. Was the person with whom I had been fighting through all this with actually the man behind it all? It was all too sick and unbelievable for me to want to comprehend. How could he have pulled it off - he didn't even speak Norwegian! The sanctuary of home became a battleground, and the lines between reality and the nightmare I was living blurred.

Collecting Evidence

After coming to the horrifying realization that Rick was most likely the mastermind behind this nightmare that I had been going through these past months, my focus immediately shifted to gathering as much evidence as possible for the police to build a case against him. I meticulously collected screenshots and messages so as to preserve fragments of the

THE NIGHTMARE DESCENDS

digital nightmare that had been inflicted upon me. I would also share these screenshots with my best friend Anette in order to safeguard against the digital deletion tactics employed by my tormentor.

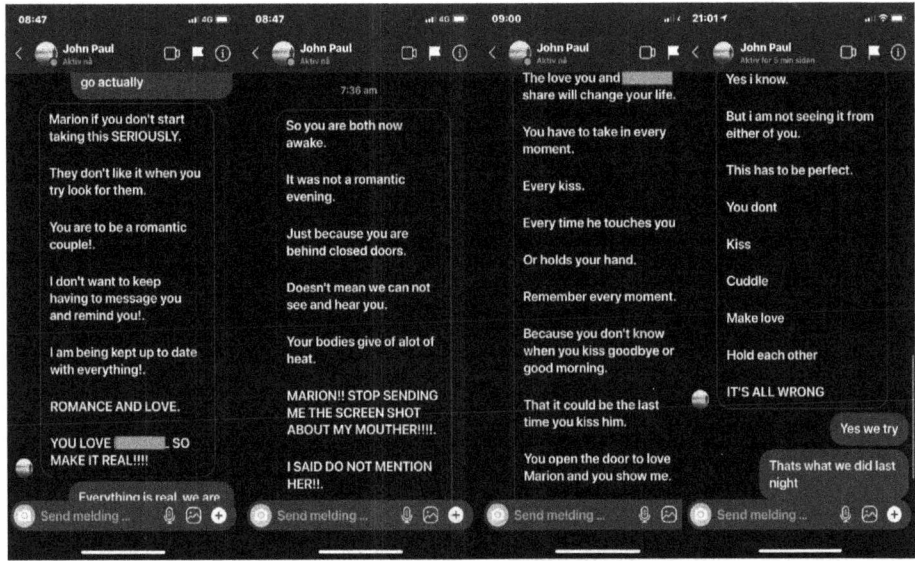

No longer feeling safe at home, I sought refuge from the claustrophobic four walls of my apartment at a nearby hotel. In the process of sifting through all of the screenshots I took, I noticed disturbing parallels between the language and spelling in the tormentor's messages and those I received from Rick. It prompted a deep yet necessary investigation into Rick's social connections, including his family, ex-girlfriends, and friends, in order to unravel the enigma of his past.

A harrowing revelation emerged from one of Rick's ex-girlfriends, recounting a traumatic tale of an invasion of privacy similar to my own experience. I found out that whilst living with his ex, she discovered that he had placed cameras in the bathroom so he could spy on her in the shower. He was also caught peeping in at her when he thought he wouldn't be noticed on multiple occasions. There was also an account of Rick throwing away her birth control pills. Possibly in an attempt to trap her. All of this painted a very disturbing picture of Rick's past. Her own horror stories mirrored my own experiences with him and solidified my suspicion that I had been sharing my living space with a deeply disturbed individual. Possibly a psychopath?

Living together was obviously no longer a viable option, so I asked a friend to help me move out. It marked a pivotal moment in my quest for safety. Rick's tearful denials and constant text messages requesting to meet with me so he could explain everything, as well as his assurances that he would never inflict harm on me seemed incongruent with the web of deception and manipulation that I was uncovering.

I decided to move in with a friend who lived in Oslo as a way of trying to distance myself from the perpetual fear that had gripped my life back in Drammen. Moving in to a new home brought with it a semblance of normalcy; yet, my distress persisted, and manifested itself in the form of threatening messages from a relentless tormentor who seemed determined to never allow me any sense of peace and relief.

Shortly after I moved in, I logged on to one of our inCruises weekly business webinars. I got genuinely excited as I prepared myself for the meeting. As people were logging on, the host, Abel, was welcoming the participants from all over the world. Suddenly I heard him say "and welcome Rick from Phoenix, Arizona." My heart sank through my stomach. I wasn't sure if I'd heard him right or if I was going crazy. I messaged my friend Margit, who was co-hosting the webinar, to ask if it was true. She confirmed it. Rick was logged on from Arizona. She also confirmed that it really was him, with his last name and profile picture. I couldn't believe it. It was the first time that I had any real evidence that Rick was behind the "Paul" Arizona profile on Instagram. I immediately asked for screenshots and saved them for evidence as well. I will never forget that feeling. Throughout the webinar, I continued to gather as much evidence as possible by saving various screenshots. I was now more determined than ever that one day he would be held responsible for his actions.

THE NIGHTMARE DESCENDS

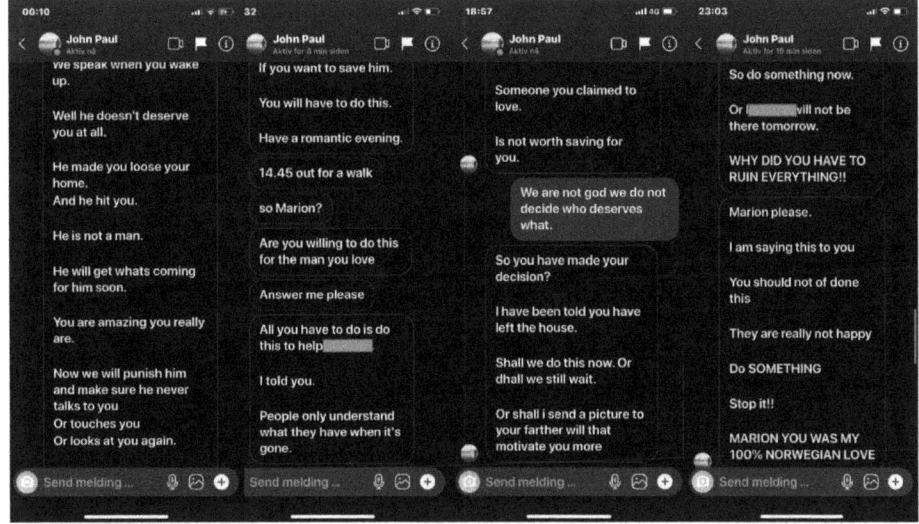

Later that same week, inCruises held a sales incentive seminar, where successful salespeople could earn a nice trip to a big mansion in Sweden. I worked very hard to earn my spot in spite of all the other drama that was going on in my life. I saw this as a fun way for me to focus on growing my business, and also a chance to get a break from everything that was going on around me.

The tormentor, now finally exposed as Rick, still wielded control over my phone and grew agitated by my interactions, particularly with Abel who at that time was the Vice-President of Communications at inCruises. He and I had started a long-distance friendship. The realization that I was moving on triggered an aggressive and vindictive response.

The weekend escape to Sweden was marred by ominous messages, like "What you are doing will have consequences." It was clear to me that another storm was brewing.

Upon my return to Oslo, I had a strong feeling that something bad was about to happen. Shortly before, a mutual friend had sent me a video from one of Rick's social media posts, in which he talks at length about him being a victim. He claimed that it had in fact been ME who had exploited HIM. He claimed that I had tricked him, ripped him off and left him destitute and homeless. This of course, couldn't have been further from the truth, but how was I supposed to respond?

I decided to contact a friend of mine and asked him to meet me at a local café. Now was not the time to be alone. Within seconds of his arrival, I started to receive more threats from Paul, whom I now knew to be Rick. He threatened to send every single one of the explicit videos and pictures of myself and him to all my family and friends, as well as release them online. I refused to be blackmailed any longer however, and told him he could do as he wished.

Within minutes, I had a torrent of messages from friends and family asking about my welfare and a thousand other questions. It was an utterly humiliating experience but after all the dust had settled, I felt a strange sense of relief. This episode not only embarrassed me but confused me as well. After all, if it was Rick doing this to me, then why would he post incriminating videos of himself punching me in the face?

I was literally going through what I once thought was my worst nightmare—having my most private and humiliating videos and pictures posted online for everyone to see. Strangely however, I was just so happy to be alive at this point that it made it that much easier for me to deal with. I also felt an odd sense of relief that there wasn't anything he had to blackmail me with any more. Still, he had exposed all my most intimate aspects of my life to all my friends and family. As messages from strangers, family, and friends flooded in, I once again began to feel vulnerable and broken.

Amidst all the chaos of these events, I found within myself a spirit of resilience. Fueled by the support of friends and family as well as a determination to salvage my own dignity, I fought to contain the fallout by encouraging everyone I knew to delete, block, and report all negative messages and posts. Despite the profound emotional pain, and my relief at having finally escaped the clutches of my tormentor by moving out, the fact that the videos were now available online for all to see meant that he no longer had that control over me. This fueled a newly found, fragile sense of hope and optimism. The journey ahead, scarred by betrayal and trauma, became a test of my will to reclaim control over my life.

THE NIGHTMARE DESCENDS

The Call from the Police

Amidst the ongoing ordeal of my explicit videos circulating online, an unexpected intrusion shattered the illusion of my escape. One night Rick, now having exposed himself, resurfaced with a barrage of menacing messages, this time from his own phone number. The messages unleashed a torrent of vitriol and threats, laden with accusations and profanity. He was beginning to come undone.

That night's events began with a relentless onslaught of calls and messages. Rick's erratic behavior soon escalated into explicit threats, accusing me of betraying him and insinuating indecent involvement with other men. The messages dripped with hatred, branding me a "whore" and vowing to destroy my life. The terrifying crescendo reached its peak when he claimed to be at a nearby park, armed with a gun and intent on ending my life.

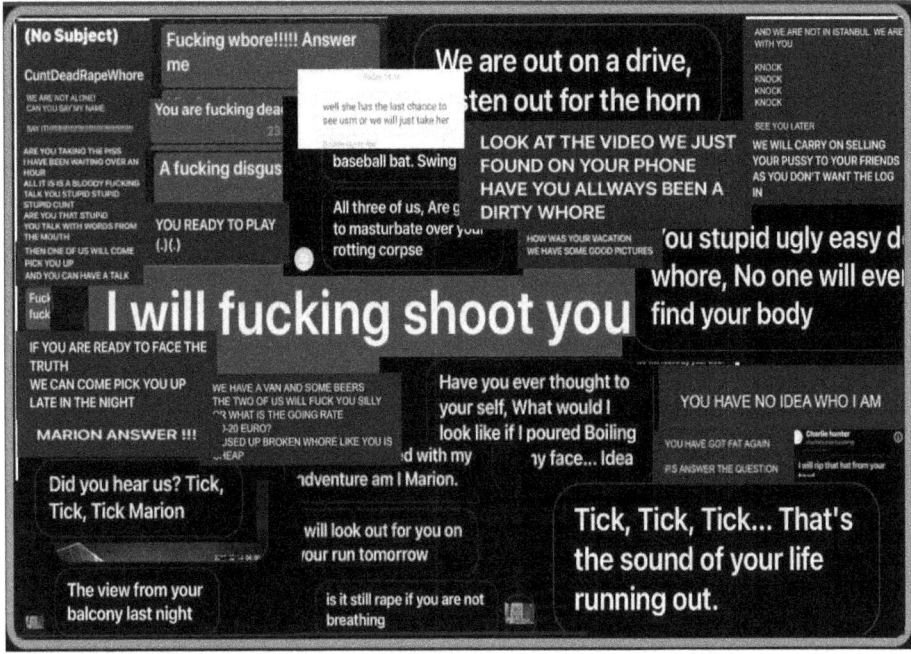

Fearing for my safety, I immediately called the police. Whilst on the phone to the police I was lying on the kitchen floor, genuinely expecting gunshots to rip through the house at any moment. Their initial response was, surprise, surprise, a big let-down. I was told that my situation was not an emergency and I would have to call their local office number!

As the night wore on, the threats intensified, resulting in me inviting my friend Fred to hang out at my place. The police eventually assured me they would stop by if they had the chance, but it did little to stop my escalating sense of alarm.

In a chilling turn of events, the police called back and confirmed that Rick had in fact called them, disclosing his full name and detailing his intent to cause me physical harm. The revelation that he claimed to be outside my door with a gun had sent shockwaves through my already frayed nerves. Yet the police adopted a wait-and-see stance—something that I still find shocking to this day—leaving me alone to grapple with the terrifying reality of a potential threat looming just outside my door.

Miraculously, the night passed without any further incident, and the threat seemed to dissipate. The following day, a visit to the police station became imperative. Armed with all the evidence I had gathered and a strong determination to finally attain justice, I recounted the harrowing tale of abuse, manipulation, rape, and threats that had consumed my life over the past few months. However, the outcome was, as always, dishearteningly swift and unsatisfying.

The police, seemed indifferent to my plight. They didn't even record my statement and offered little in terms of tangible action. I was simply told to write to an email and fill out a form which I suspect got lost in the endless bureaucracy of the system. The urgency I felt clashed with the dismissive response from the authorities that greeted my pleas for intervention. The criminal acts, including the release of explicit videos and physical assaults I endured, seemed meaningless and dismissed by only being documented in a police report.

I decided to stay in Oslo for a while longer, but the shadow of Rick's influence lingered on. The relentless barrage of messages continued, demonstrating an unsettling tenacity and resilience that I feel could have been put to much better use elsewhere in his life.

THE NIGHTMARE DESCENDS

After about a month in Oslo, I moved back to Drammen, the city where it all started. My stay in Oslo had been a quick solution to get away from my old apartment. Now I was back in Drammen, staying with my dear friend Raymond, whom I had met the previous year.

Raymond is special. He's the type of friend that we all wish we had. He's one of the funniest guys I know and is always willing to reach out and help others. Aside from that, I know Raymond will never fall in love with me because he bats for the other team. I was so happy to be there with him and I felt that much safer knowing that he was there for me.

By this time, the gyms had opened up again, and so I could get back to my usual exercise routine. Every evening I would walk down the streets to my gym and think about those recent days when I felt so trapped that I couldn't even find the will to leave my front door. Yet at times, I still felt watched and the relentless messages kept coming in about my life choices and my daily movements.

Not long after I moved in with Raymond, things took a dark turn, when on the morning of my 25th birthday, someone decided to send me a very memorable birthday present. An 'unknown' person called in a fake bomb threat to Raymond's apartment. The police responded diligently and with force. It was such a surreal and crazy experience for both myself and Raymond and caused a lot of tension as you can imagine. This "swatting" incident was clearly intended to both intimidate and manipulate me into contact, and added to my on-going trauma.

We received confirmation that Rick was the person behind all this, when, later that day we saw a newspaper article showing Rick being arrested in relation to the incident. Rick was brought in for questioning but he was released. The legal system had once again failed to hold him accountable for any of his actions. All I could get was a restraining order, which offered little comfort at that point.

The ongoing fear and uncertainty left me wondering if the legal system would ever deliver justice and put an end to the relentless campaign of harassment and intimidation that had become such a big part of my life. The journey towards justice was fraught with lots of red tape and systemic shortcomings, highlighting the challenges that victims face in navigating what I believe to be a flawed legal landscape.

Moving to My Parents

Right before Christmas 2020, I moved back home to my parents' house. I couldn't stay in Oslo any longer. It had come to a point where I not only felt like I was putting myself in danger, but also Raymond and the sweet 80-year-old lady who owned the house we were staying at. I had gotten the restraining order and it may have kept him away to some extent, but I continued to receive messages 24/7 from various unknown email addresses and different Facebook accounts. I never received something that I could readily take to the police and say, "Hey, I got this message from a stranger, but I know it's him", though.

The harassment persisted. I felt increasingly unsafe and wasn't entirely sure if moving to my parents' house had been the right decision after all. Many of his previous threats had involved my family, and I didn't want to expose them to any more danger. It did however, seem like my only viable option at the time.

My sister came to pick me up from the station, and we loaded all my belongings, including my little black cat, Bob, and headed to my parents' house.

Back in my old home, I felt the need to keep constant surveillance of the house, keeping an eye on both front and back doors for personal safety. Sleeping in my old bedroom felt risky, as I feared he might find a way in and do harm to my parents or my sister. As a result, I spent most nights curled up on the sofa, unable to relax or sleep.

Rick's tactics then evolved. He started trying to scam me financially and sent a massive number of sex toys to my parents' house. I would receive email after email from the bank accepting or declining my requests for a loan. Thankfully I noticed all these attempts quickly enough and contacted the banks before anything was done. It was clear though, that he had all the necessary private information needed to create big problems for me financially. After a while of this going on, I successfully put myself on the "do not loan money list," even though I was told it might affect my future ability to gain credit. It was however, my only real option at the time, and the only way to make sure my bank accounts were secure.

During this period, I meticulously documented all the ongoing events, collecting screenshots of messages, including those from Rick himself. These messages played a crucial role in providing evidence for the police. Simultaneously, I received unsettling emails, some expressing anger and others ominously claiming, "We know where you are." Pictures of my parents' house and the surrounding area were often sent, adding to the paranoia. The sender of the emails always referred to himself as "we" as if there were several people involved.

One morning, I even woke up to a chilling photo captioned, "This was your balcony last night."

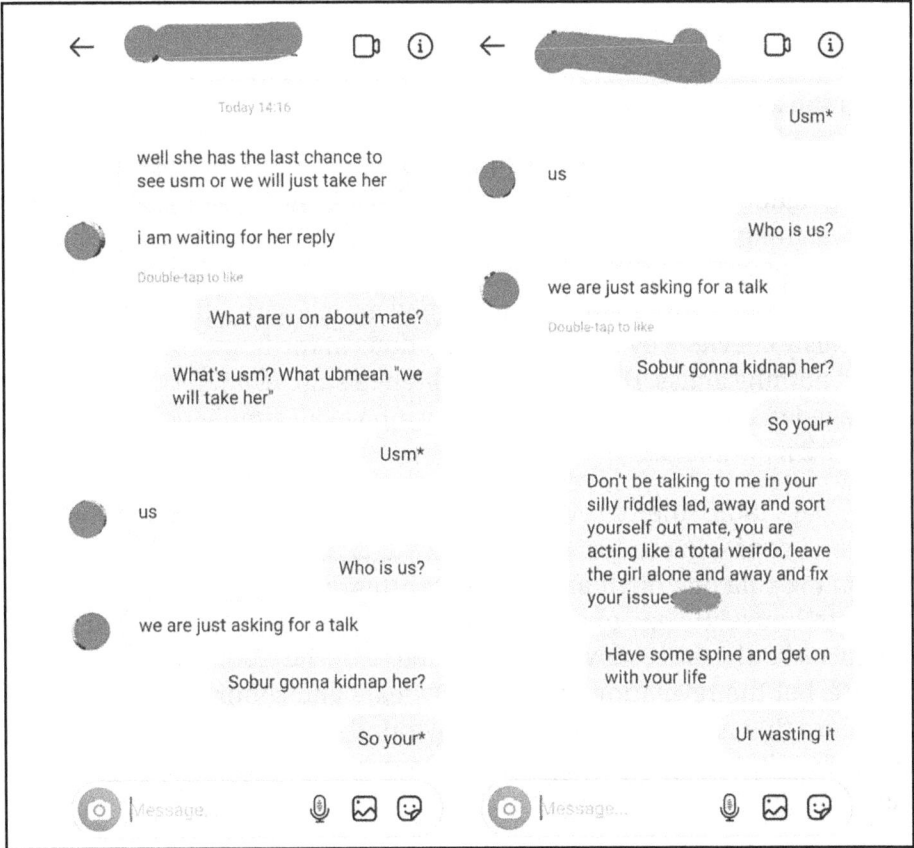

While the messages from fake users continued to persist, Rick updated his Facebook story with pictures from what looked like my hometown, which proved his nearby presence. He also kept posting stories which hinted at wanting to see me dead. A common friend of ours had seen these very same stories and reached out to me. I told him everything about what had been going on, and he decided to contact Rick directly in order to get his side of the story. Rick informed him that "they" simply wanted to meet and talk with me, and that I had one chance to comply before "they" would kidnap me.

Nightly messages foretold ominous plans. Threats of "them" coming to pick me up and demanding I go to meet them alone persisted. The onslaught was relentless, 24/7. One night, Rick's messages took on another strange turn, when he expressed his yearning to see me, his nervousness, and his need for a drink before meeting. This was one of the few times he admitted to being behind all this. Although tempted, common sense prevailed as I felt sick at the prospect of ever seeing him in person again. I refrained from responding.

One evening not long after, while watching TV on the sofa, an eerie feeling suddenly gripped me — I had a terrifying sense that someone was watching me from outside. My fear escalated when the door handle began rattling loudly. I became so paralyzed with fear that it must have taken me minutes to finally react. I armed myself with a fire poker before cautiously checking every window and door in the house but, thankfully, found nothing amiss. Despite my heightened state of anxiety, I eventually managed to convince myself that it must have all simply been a product of my own paranoia.

A few days later, Anette revealed to me a shocking piece of information. Rick had confessed to her via text message, that he had been watching me on the sofa one night and had even attempted to gain entry in to my parents' house! He had only failed to do so due to the doors and windows being locked! I have never understood why he confessed all this to Anette, but the revelation validated my fears and confirmed his physical presence that night. I believed this newfound evidence would strengthen my case with the police, especially given his repeated breaches of the restraining order which included text messaging.

On another occasion, I received a cryptic message from a strange Facebook account. This supposedly Norwegian man claimed that he had been Rick's roommate for a short time, but that on the morning of January 1st Rick had committed suicide by hanging himself. I immediately became suspicious of the communication because his Norwegian was obviously someone using Google translate. He went on to state that Rick had left a letter for me and that he would like to meet with me in order to hand it over to me personally. Sensing another trap, I obviously refused.

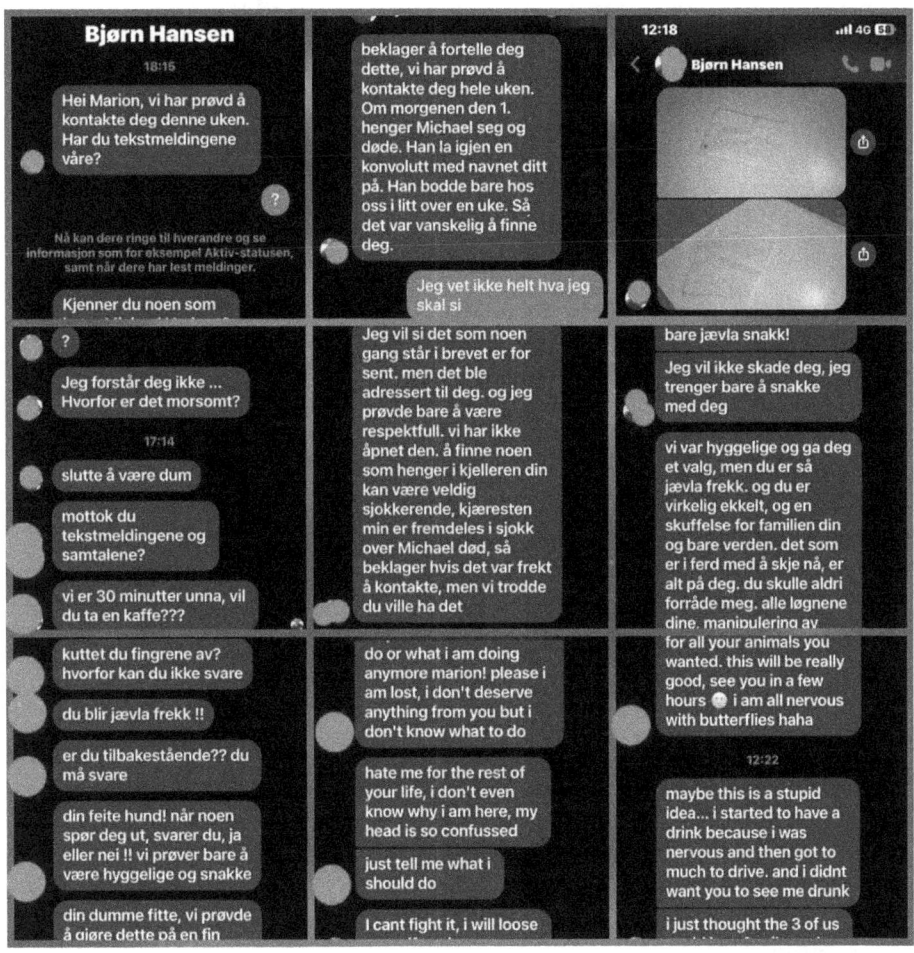

Anette reached out to the police and they confirmed to us that Rick was alive and well and that this was obviously an attempt to fake his own death. Despite confirming the deception, the police refused to press the matter further and remained unresponsive to my inquiries, leaving me with a lot of mounting frustration.

After putting further pressure on the police, they started requiring Rick to register at a police station three times a week, as a consequence of violating his restraining order on multiple occasions. Despite this positive piece of progress, my trust in the police and legal system had by now been shattered beyond repair, and I began considering alternative ways I could escape my predicament.

Trouble in Turkey

In order to gain some distance from my troubles and clear my head a little, I decided to take a trip to Turkey to meet up with Abel, a man with whom I had started to have frequent long-distance contact with. It would be an opportunity to break free from the relentless messages and threats. However, even on the other side of Europe I couldn't escape my relentless pursuer in yet another disturbing episode.

Before embarking on my travels, I had to navigate COVID-related requirements, including obtaining a COVID test in Oslo. During this preparation phase, messages continued to flood in, notifying me of my intentions. Despite this, I pressed on with my plans for Turkey. However, a booking mishap at the airport delayed my initial departure. Undeterred, I secured a new flight a few days later. Whilst waiting for my new flight, the messages continued to escalate in creepiness, including details about my flight, destination, and stay. "They" claimed to be at the airport watching me and somehow knew that I was having a beer—they were going to have a beer too!

Arriving in Turkey, I met Abel in person for the first time but the messages persisted, hinting that someone was watching us, informing us of our whereabouts, and even promising a "gift" on our door - a promise that went unfulfilled.

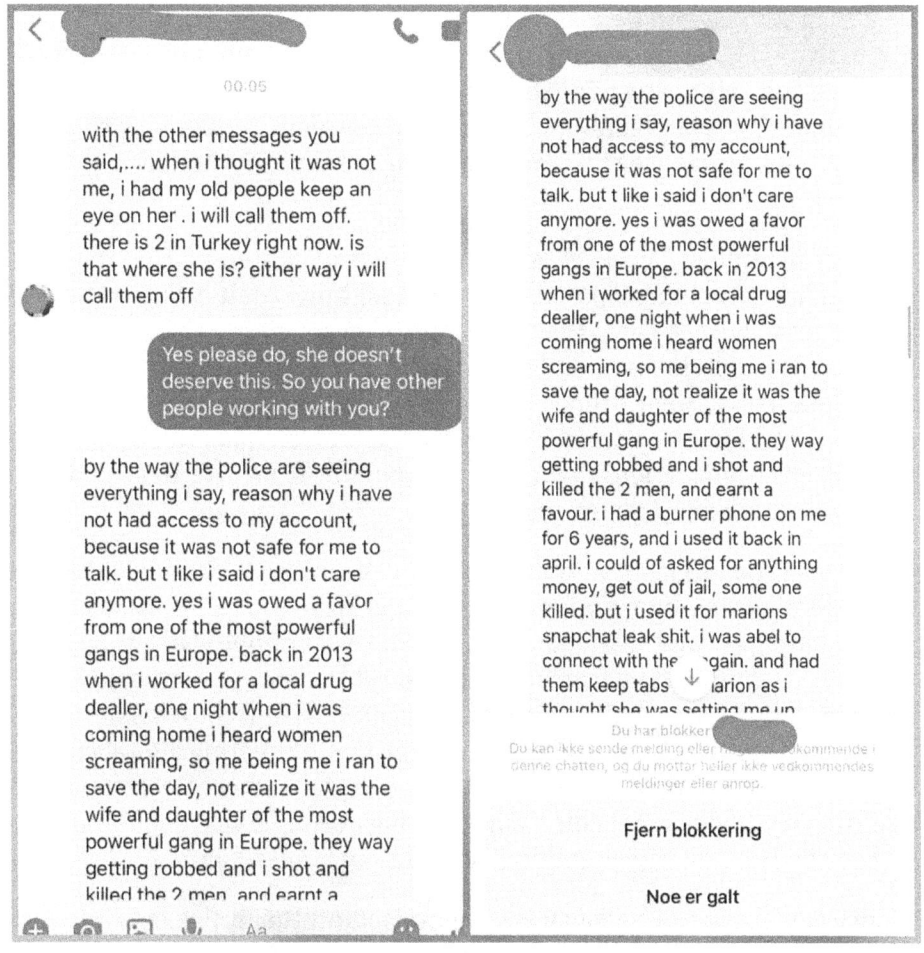

As we settled into the hotel, I continued to receive an onslaught of bizarre messages. Abel had met Rick through some of the company webinars we had been on before all the craziness really began to unfold. Rick was very well aware of who Abel was and he was also very much aware that he had started to become a part of my life. Abel, for his part, was also well informed about everything that had been going on up to this point.

On one particular afternoon in Turkey we had another team webinar. It didn't take long for Abel to notice that Rick had logged on to the webinar with a Turkey IP address. Unbelievable! Abel messaged Rick asking him if he was in Turkey, and he responded that he was. Rick had obviously made a massive mistake by logging on with his actual name and a Turkey IP address, and this corresponded with the fact that I was getting messages from other people claiming to be in Turkey who threatened to harm me. By now it was clear to me that he was becoming totally unhinged and desperate.

During our time in Turkey, I often found myself contemplating the need for a significant change, particularly as it no longer felt safe to return to my hometown in Norway, the town where I grew up in and where I once had a sense of belonging and familiarity. Everything had changed. The relentless harassment from Rick, coupled with the spread of videos and pictures, had forever altered how people perceived me. I felt as though I had lost my identity, and that people would never be able to see past all the chaos that had engulfed me.

Once I returned to my hometown, I no longer felt comfortable going out to familiar places or meeting with friends in public. I withdrew from social activities, and avoided the mall and any public gatherings. The relentless scrutiny had transformed me into someone unrecognizable and the town that I had once loved became a source of anxiety and discomfort. It was at this point that I began contemplating a total change of scenery, and Mallorca emerged as a potential refuge. Despite all the daunting challenges that come with moving abroad, I yearned for a fresh start away from all the judgmental eyes of my hometown.

A pervasive sense of betrayal by the police and the entire legal system of my own country, weighed heavily on my mind. Despite months of fighting and enduring countless traumatic experiences, the lack of any tangible action from the authorities left me feeling abandoned. Their ongoing response to all of my enquiries was always, "We are unable to say anything further at this time." I confronted them, questioning what more needed to happen in order for them to intervene. The lack of any significant progress or communication further fueled my frustration, leaving me in the dark about Rick's whereabouts and any legal proceedings. I had always thought the whole point of a police force was to keep citizens safe.

THE NIGHTMARE DESCENDS

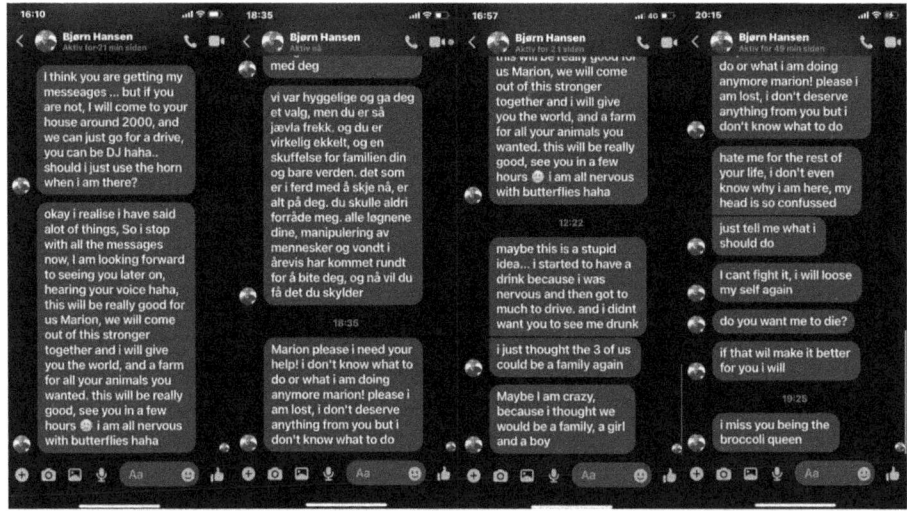

Amidst all this turmoil, the mysterious "Norwegian" Facebook user who claimed that Rick had killed himself, kept insisting upon delivering the letter, but conflicting information soon added to the confusion. I was eventually informed by Annette that Rick had told her he had been taken for a medical assessment and was found to be unfit for trial. The police remained elusive on the matter however, so I questioned why they would be involved in discussions with him without considering my perspective, the victim in this case. I never got a proper answer although I was informed someone would be in contact.

Rick's social media posts over the preceding months suggested that he had been in and out of mental institutions in Norway, adding to the uncertainty. The dissonance between what Rick communicated and what the police disclosed deepened my sense of helplessness and disappointment.

A major factor in my decision to move abroad stemmed from the complete erosion of my life in Norway. I had lost my home, my job, and a substantial part of my financial stability. Fears of judgment from a community fueled by rumors and misconceptions further pushed me to consider emigrating, even though it seemed a daunting task to rebuild my life amidst the remnants of all the chaos that had unfolded. The decision to move became a necessity, a chance to escape the ruins of a life that had crumbled and find solace elsewhere on a distant shore.

After three months of living at home, I made up my mind that I was going to move back to Mallorca. First though, Abel and I had another business trip planned for Turkey. Whilst waiting at the airport I received a phone call from the police for the first time in months. They stated that Rick was too mentally unstable for them to hold him and that they had decided to deport him from Norway. I was heartbroken and started crying because I feared that he might go back to Mallorca. The lack of communication from the police thus far had made me assume that Rick would either be staying in Norway or be made aware to British authorities. Now I knew that I was very much mistaken.

CHAPTER 5
New life, New Country

New Job, New Beginning

As soon as I got off the plane at Palma airport, I felt a sense of relief and well-being that I hadn't felt in ages. In preparation for my arrival, I had reached out to an old friend who graciously offered me temporary accommodation until I could find my feet again. Eager to rebuild my life, I wasted no time in searching for employment. Fortunately, another friend, who happened to be Swedish, had connections with some other Swedish individuals who ran a bar in Magaluf. They were in need of additional staff, and after a swift job interview, I found myself employed almost immediately.

The establishment I joined was a family business, owned by two cousins and frequented by their sister, mother, and father. It comprised of both a laid-back bar and a restaurant. This familial atmosphere provided me with a sense of stability and support during my initial days back on the island. However, amidst all the optimism of a fresh start, I began to hear rumors circulating around Magaluf that Rick was planning on returning to Mallorca.

Wary of the impending threat, I decided to confide in my new colleagues about my situation. The sister of one of the owners was genuinely concerned for my safety and urged me to contact the Guardia Civil (Police) in order to inform them of the looming danger. She and I visited the police station together, where she translated my story to the officers. I shared with them all the evidence from my phone and, to my genuine surprise, they reacted with a real sense of urgency.

Not a moment too soon either. The gravity of the situation became apparent when I learned that Rick had made plans for his imminent arrival on the island. The police took my case extremely seriously though, and provided me with 24-hour close-by protection. They accompanied me everywhere I went, ensuring my safety during daily activities like grocery shopping, going to the gym, or even relaxing at the beach. At work, a police car remained parked right across the street from me, attesting to their efficiency and constant vigilance.

On my part, I had to appear in court with my lawyer in order to present my case to the judge and request a restraining order. The court proceedings went smoothly and efficiently, the judge acknowledged the severity of the situation and granted a restraining order against Rick. Reflecting on this challenging period in my life, I recall a poignant moment where, just before entering the courtroom, I was placed in a room filled with other women all of whom had experienced some sort of domestic violence themselves. I could see the visible pain and distress written across their eyes and faces. Some of them were sobbing relentlessly. This experience deeply affected me, and highlighted the fact that my case was in no way an isolated incident and that my struggles were shared by plenty of other survivors. This reinforced my belief in the importance of breaking down the taboos which have surrounded the issue of domestic abuse for such a long time.

Looking back on this time in my life, this episode served as the catalyst for a change of direction and solidified my resolve to overcome all challenges and share my story with others who might be enduring similar hardships.

Strange Things Happening

During this period, I transitioned from staying at a hotel to moving in with my boss's family due to financial constraints. The 24-hour police protection was scaled back, and I was no longer accompanied constantly, although I did receive periodic check ups. Even so, my safety concerns persisted, especially after a break-in occurred in the storage room behind the house I was staying at. Although nothing was stolen, the incident did raise suspicions, and the police, convinced it was Rick's doing, recommended that we install an alarm system just in case.

The unsettling sense of being watched during my walks home from work persisted. This heightened state of paranoia stemmed from the fear that Rick, now aware of my exact location, might follow me home one evening. Thankfully, nothing happened during these walks, but never-the-less the dreaded sense of unease I had tried so hard to distance myself from returned.

One sunny afternoon, to my utter horror, I spotted Rick sitting across the road from the bar where I worked, having a beer with a friend. I became panicked and a bit hysterical. One of my workmates called the police, and they promptly removed him, enforcing the restraining order. This only marked the first instance of him violating the new order. Shortly afterwards, a similar incident occurred, leading to another courtroom appearance for me. To their credit, this time the court informed me that if he violated the restraining order just once more, he would face imprisonment.

This development stirred mixed emotions within me. While relieved at the prospect of him finally facing consequences, the fear intensified. I was worried that, aware of the potential for imprisonment, he might resort to more covert and dangerous means to harm me. The ongoing tension and paranoia was relentless, making my nightly walks home from work an even more vulnerable and harrowing experience.

Amidst all of this, disturbing rumors about myself that were obviously started by Rick began circulating around my new social circles. I was told by former mutual friends that I was in fact the psychopath. They accused me of manipulating Rick into engaging and filming sexual acts for my own financial gain. They said that I was the one who had forced him into exploitative situations, and then left him homeless after taking all his money. These hurtful rumors spread quickly in the small town, causing me considerably more emotional distress. Some people even came up to physically confront me and asked how I was capable of doing such things. How could I hurt him in such a way? Can you imagine how that made me feel after everything that he had put me through?

The lies were contradicted by a substantial amount of evidence which supported my side of the story, including Rick's own threatening posts on social media in which he had alluded to his intention to kill me. He had also posted about several serial killers such as Ted Bundy whom he seemed to idolize.

Navigating this intricate web of rumors, threats, and legal battles became increasingly challenging, adding a certain layer of complexity to an already traumatic experience. How much more would I have to endure? Was Rick done with me or did he have more in store? There was no way of really knowing although the months ahead would answer that question.

CHAPTER 6
Aftershock

Trying to Rise Above

The prolonged stress of constantly being in fight-or-flight mode had begun to take a serious toll on my mental health. Despite being in a relatively safe environment with police protection, my mind struggled to shift away from constant vigilance. Paranoia had become a pervasive presence, causing me to overreact with intense distress to ordinary everyday situations, such as a car or stranger on the street passing by.

The next major struggle to deal with, was the abrupt disruption of my sleep patterns. Due to being overcome by anxiety and an ever-present sense of nervousness, I found myself unable to sleep for more than an hour at a stretch. I eventually realized the urgency of addressing the state of my mental well-being, so I decided to return home in order to reach out and seek help from the health services back in Norway.

In the lead up to my first session I had experienced five days of almost no sleep. During that first encounter at the doctor's I almost immediately completely broke down and told my doctor all about my traumatic experiences. To his credit, he quickly recognized the severity of the situation and sent an emergency message to the district mental health unit. He also prescribed me with sleeping pills and anxiety medication, in order to get me through the anxious wait for the promised care from the relevant mental health authorities.

Unfortunately, the mental health system in Norway proved to be an inefficient series of roadblocks. After a while, I received a letter stating that my case was not considered an emergency, and that they don't deal with trauma of this kind. Frustrated and desperate for assistance, I contacted them again only to be told to apply for general counseling, which might take months. Once again, I felt neglected and let down by my own home country.

Feeling cornered and with no discernable solution on the horizon, I made the difficult decision to return to Mallorca, despite the daunting uncertainty of Rick's whereabouts.

Eventually, I did receive a call from a woman at the Norwegian psychiatric office who offered to put me in contact with a therapist for online sessions. By this time however, although appreciative of the offer, I felt that this wasn't the tye of specialized help that I needed.

Reflecting on my experiences with what I consider to be a flawed mental health system, has since prompted me to contemplate ways that I could contribute to real positive change, and raise awareness of the issues surrounding victim support. Despite the challenges ahead, I hope that my story will highlight the importance of acknowledging the psychological toll of traumatic experiences and the importance of seeking the appropriate support.

The Spanish Doctor

After navigating a labyrinth of bureaucratic challenges in Norway, it became clear to me that the system there couldn't offer the assistance I so desperately needed. The disheartening response was essentially a suggestion to consult the internet and try to cure all my troubles with a healthy dose of 'self-research'. By disregarding the sheer depth of psychological trauma embedded by my quite frankly terrifying, life-threatening experience, the Norwegian authorities dismissed the severity of my case, leaving me feeling vulnerable and alone in my struggles.

Upon my return to Mallorca I rented my own apartment in the capital, Palma, a place far removed from the chaos of Magaluf. Now, armed with some stability and a positive attitude, I decided to give it another shot. Hoping that the system in Mallorca would come through for me once again. In the spring of 2023, I reached out to my Swedish friend, the same friend that had been there for me before and had offered me her home as a refuge. She was now working at a doctor's office, and in a matter of minutes, she responded to my enquiry with a reassuring, "Come here, we will help you." The next day, I found myself at the doctor's office, discussing my ordeal. Although therapy wasn't immediately offered, the doctor did prescribe medications for my anxiety and sleep issues.

The mere act of seeking help and getting some prescribed medication felt like a big step forward and marked an important turning point in my life. Unlike my experiences in Norway, where I felt neglected and unsupported, the Spanish doctor welcomed me warmly. There was no judgment, shame, or awkwardness. My problems and feelings felt accepted and understood. This supportive environment, coupled with regular check-ins from my friend at the doctor's office, created a kind of mental safety net, which allowed me to freely share my feelings and struggles without fear of judgment.

Even though I do believe my doctor back in Norway had done his best, the differences between the Norwegian and Spanish healthcare systems soon became apparent. Not only did the Spanish doctor demonstrate genuine care and prescribe me the appropriate medications, he also provided the ongoing support that I so badly needed. Regular check-ups, prescription renewals, and offers to discuss my progress showcased a genuine commitment to my overall well-being, for which I will be forever grateful.

Whilst my long journey to complete recovery is still ongoing, the improvement in my mental state was palpable within the first couple of months. Finally feeling seen and supported, I embarked on a path towards self-healing, shedding the layers of anxiety, paranoia, and sleeplessness that had haunted me for so many years. The Spanish doctor's unwavering support not only aided my recovery but also demonstrated to me the important and transformative impact that comes from a compassionate and genuinely considerate healthcare professional.

Creating Healthy Habits

With a new sense of empowerment and a feeling that I was finally getting some of the help that I needed, a sense of relief washed over me. I was no longer grappling with the burden of my struggles on my own. Having someone genuinely there for me allowed me the necessary mental space to breathe, to focus on myself, and to contemplate how to embark on the future journey of healing. No longer haunted by the constant worry of "What am I going to do?" or "Who can I talk to?" I had found a renewed sense of optimism and purpose.

One of my initial steps towards self-care was hitting the gym. The significance of physical activity when dealing with mental health issues, cannot be overstated. Stepping into the gym for the first time in ages, I could feel my stress dissipate, and with each visit, my mental well-being improved. The gym became my sanctuary, a place where I could not only engage in physical exercise but also reclaim a sense of control over my thoughts and emotions.

In addition to gym sessions, I embraced the therapeutic benefits of nature. Whilst I was initially a bit reluctant, I started incorporating walks and hikes into my routine and attempted to connect more deeply with nature, although it was by no means an instant revelation. As I delved further into the healing process, I discovered the concept of "grounding"—the theory that direct connection of your body to the earth, for instance by walking barefoot on grass or sand, promotes a sense of mental well-being. At this point, I wasn't totally "out of the woods" (no pun intended) because the feelings of being watched or attacked at any moment were still very much a part of my life.

Walking in the woods, surrounded by nature, I found a tranquil escape, a place where I could feel my stress practically melt away, and I could focus on personal growth. Often, I brought my notebook along in order to write down and visualize my thoughts, using the time for self-reflection. Whether journaling, expressing gratitude, problem-solving, setting goals, planning my day, or indulging in creative thinking, the natural setting became the ideal environment in which to nurture my mind and soul.

Digital Detox

Before I can settle down and begin to write, I intentionally turn my phone off and keep it out of sight. In today's hyper-connected world, our digital devices serve as a constant series of distractions such as endless messages, emails, social media updates, and the incessant stream of news, which I have always found to be particularly anxiety-inducing. Whenever I feel overwhelmed by this electronic cacophony, I retreat to the woods and put my phone aside. This immediately feels like I am creating my own sanctuary - a refuge where all the noises of the outside world fade away. The stresses of needing to be somewhere or promptly responding to someone dissipate, and I find peace in the simplicity of disconnecting from it all.

Modern society is very much reliant on the internet and keeping everyone online and connected. What many people don't realise, is that our phones are designed to keep us reliant and engaged as well as constantly store and send information about us to third parties. Even during the seemingly harmless act of scrolling through posts on social media, your phone sends out information about how much time you spend focusing on each post. Social media in general, is all deliberately designed to keep our brains constantly distracted, processing mostly meaningless information without us fully realizing the toll it takes on our mental capabilities. It is only when I am away from the digital realm, that I can truly be alone with my thoughts. It's in these moments of disconnecting from the virtual world that I regain a sense of control over myself.

Reflecting on my past struggles with anxiety, I acknowledge that, I initially used my phone as a distraction. The notion of sitting in nature and confronting my own thoughts seemed far too overwhelming. It's a sentiment shared by many who view the idea of solitary contemplation amidst nature as potentially stress-inducing. However, the more I have embraced this practice, the more I have come to realize its truly transformative power.

While researching, I came across an intriguing insight on the impact of screen time on our brains. When we gaze at our mobile phones or other 'blue light' screens, our brain releases dopamine, the "feel good" chemical that impacts on our mood, brain function and sleep cycle. Studies have been carried out that show many children who are hooked on gaming, when given brain scans, display brain activity akin to that of a person on cocaine. The brain craves more and more of this natural high, which fosters an addiction to our devices. The incessant stream of content on social media, driven by all its algorithms, is intentionally designed to control our thoughts and behaviour.

By intentionally stepping away from screens and immersing myself in the serenity of nature, I have found comfort in my own thoughts and regained control over my mental space. This simple act of disconnecting, even for a brief moment, serves as a powerful tool to break the cycle of constant digital engagement. Moreover, as I have researched the intricacies of stalking, I have come to recognize the weaponization of technology against victims. This has further reinforced my belief in the importance of reclaiming control over our minds through periodic digital detoxes.

Travel

Throughout the course of those challenging years, I was lucky enough to have embarked on numerous journeys, to all the different corners of the globe. From the vibrant streets of Miami to the rich cultural tapestry of Mexico, the ancient wonders of Greece, and even the serene landscapes of my home country of Norway. I've wandered through the enchanting streets of Paris, explored the historical allure of Turkey, and encountered the dynamic vibes of Cyprus.

In the aftermath of my harrowing experience with a real-life psycho, it became paramount for me not to allow him to dictate my thoughts, my future, or my everyday life. Traveling emerged as a powerful tool, a means to break free from the shackles of my comfort zone, which, post-trauma, had shrunk considerably. I'm not trying to say it's been easy because I still have moments when the mundane task of leaving the house to run simple errands, such as overcoming that five-minute walk to the supermarket, becomes daunting and seems like an insurmountable challenge.

The beauty of travel lies not just in exploring new landscapes but in connecting with the diverse tapestry of humanity. Venturing beyond my comfort zone meant more than just a trip to the supermarket; it was about leaving my home, my city, and sometimes even my country. It was a conscious decision to expose myself to new experiences, new people, and new challenges. The encounters with people from different backgrounds, each with their own story, goals, and ambitions opened my eyes to the vast spectrum of human existence.

Traveling has been a catalyst for personal growth. It has forced me to confront discomfort, uncertainty, and fear head-on, instead of succumbing to the comfort of my sofa and the safety of a familiar routine. I chose to step into the unknown, and the lessons I've learned during these adventures have been instrumental in my journey towards healing and reclaiming my life.

The mindset of a stalker revolves around manipulation, control, and isolation. The act of leaving one's comfort zone and building connections is a direct contradiction to the stalker's objectives. By immersing myself in different cultures, languages, and customs, I dismantled the power the stalker held over me. Travel became a mechanism not just to explore the world but to rebuild my life myself, one connection at a time. It's one of the reasons why I'm sharing my story in this book— to testify about the transformative power that travel and human connection can have in overcoming adversity.

Healthy Relationships and Trust

Recently, my book writing coach, Dr. Denis Cauvier, shared a profound quotation from his mentor, Bill Gibson: "Time plus genuine sincere interest creates trust, and that trust is the cornerstone of every true healthy relationship." This deeply resonates with me, especially considering the tumultuous journey I've been on.

In the midst of my story, in which my trust has been repeatedly shattered by a deranged stalker, I found myself having to learn how to rebuild trust and confidence again. One pivotal figure in this journey was Abel, whom I had met right in the middle of all the chaos. We were initially introduced through shared professional interests in the inCruises business, before we connected virtually, with Abel leading webinars that I avidly followed. His demeanor and approach gave me a sense of the person he was.

As we started conversing, Abel went beyond the professional realm, expressing a genuine interest in understanding my life and emotions. This mature and supportive engagement, a departure from my past experiences, caught me off guard in the most positive way. Daily phone conversations became the norm, bridging the gap between virtual and real connections.

The true test of trust arrived when I planned that trip to Turkey. Initially, I had intended to stay with a friend. When my friend had to cancel, I found myself contemplating whether or not to reach out to Abel, whom I had never met in person. Despite my initial hesitation, I took the plunge, and to my surprise, he not only invited me to stay with him but demonstrated a sincere empathy and understanding that further solidified the trust we were building. Abel has told me that he'll never forget when he saw me in person for the first time on that crazy trip to Turkey. He opened the door and said that I looked like a lost, confused, beautiful little puppy. It was a special moment and we connected instantly. He says that when we go weeks or sometimes months without seeing each other due to our long-distance relationship, he's always shocked at how beautiful I am each time he sees me. He's so adorable!

Reflecting on this journey, I've come to realize the importance of trusting one's instincts, a lesson learned through the hardships of my past. Abel's genuine interest and consistent support has served as a beacon, teaching me to not only trust others but, more crucially, myself. My conversations with Abel also highlight the significance of self-worth in relationships. Like all relationships, our relationship isn't perfect—far from it. We have good days and bad days. And maintaining a long-distance relationship with someone from a completely different culture and background comes with its challenges. But somehow we make it work.

Before, I was too quick to trust, a trait stemming from a lack of self-worth and a desire for external validation. I allowed people into my life without understanding their true intentions. Now, having faced the darkest depths of my struggles, I recognize the need to value myself and demand the respect that I deserve.

Denis shared a concept about loving and protecting people and I think that struck a chord with me: If you love someone or something, of course you protect it. But the same principle applies to self-love - when you truly value yourself, you won't allow others to treat you poorly. Trusting others becomes a natural extension of trusting oneself.

In essence, the journey of rebuilding trust after facing betrayal involves understanding and valuing one's self-worth. It's about listening to your instincts, recognizing red flags, and surrounding yourself with those who appreciate and respect your true value. Through this profound transformation, I've learned that the cornerstone of every healthy relationship begins with the trust you build within yourself.

Ups and Downs: Navigating Life's Rollercoaster

I want readers to understand that despite having overcome my stalker, my life these days isn't a perpetual stroll through fields of flowers. Even though embracing a gym routine and finding moments of joy will help with the healing process, life after trauma is marked by a constant series of ups and downs. The challenges persist, a reminder that the echoes of past experiences can cast long shadows on even the sunniest of days.

On some days, the weight of my experiences resurface, demanding an extra measure of effort to find the strength to persevere through my daily routines or to partake in social interactions. The simple act of stepping outside can morph into a battle against the lingering impact of the past. On these down days, the challenges seem insurmountable, but acknowledging these struggles exist is an essential part of the healing process.

For me, the starting point for overcoming these challenges begins with the simple act of opening your door and leaving the house. Taking that initial step, even if it feels tentative and slow, serves as the catalyst for further progress. The journey to the gym becomes more than physical; it transforms into a therapeutic odyssey, helping you to overcome any initial resistance. Nevertheless, there are still instances when, despite reaching the gym's entrance, the prospect of stepping inside seems like an insurmountable hurdle.

In those moments, self-talk emerges as a potent tool. Personally, I remind myself of the genuine love I have for the gym, the positive impact it consistently has on my mental well-being, and the profound sense of accomplishment that follows a gym session. Self-talk helps me to break through any negativity I have. It's a conscious effort to shift the focus away from the expectation of a workout on to the tangible benefits of the investment in yourself.

Crucially, realizing that it doesn't have to be an all-or-nothing scenario is pivotal. Acknowledging that some days are inherently tougher than others becomes a mantra—***progress over perfection***. Even a brief, 10-minute workout on challenging days still stands as a victory, a testament to resilience. The significance lies in making the effort in the first place. The simple act of stepping into the gym, can contribute immeasurably to feeling better than lazily succumbing to inertia on the couch.

CHAPTER 7
Writing the Future

What I am most concerned about these days is knowing that despite being exposed and somewhat punished, Rick is still out there and could very well strike again. This fear isn't just about my own vulnerability; it is very much extended to the possibility of another unsuspecting individual falling prey to his sick predilections. The haunting thought that he is now focusing his unwanted attention on someone else, and that they might be enduring the same anguish I once did, has become a profound source of motivation to me. I consider myself extremely lucky to have survived his obsession, but perhaps his next object of desire won't be so lucky.

The motivation to share my story and embark on the challenging task of writing a book— which has been made even more formidable by English not being my first language—arises from the profound frustration I felt whilst navigating the complexities of the bureaucratic legal system. The inadequate response from law enforcement to my predicament, combined with a desire to address a broader societal issue, has spurred me to consider ways in which I can make a meaningful impact on society.

Writing this book wasn't an easy decision. It required overcoming my own lack of confidence and vulnerability, whilst exposing my intimate struggles to a public audience. Yet, the potential to make a difference, coupled with constant news stories and documentaries about victims of stalking, made it obvious to me that I needed to get my story out there. It seems that every week I'm made aware of this ever-growing crisis. Stories of women dying or suffering at the hands of sick individuals. Even in my country of Norway, I've heard multiple stories from women who reached out to law enforcement for help time and time again, only to be failed by the system— and who have ended up dead as a result of the indifference. Having been failed by the system myself and understanding what that's like, motivated me to write this book. What about those countless others who are suffering in silence, too scared to come forward?

Although writing a book is typically a solitary journey, I have always been aware that I have not been alone in this endeavor. My editor Alex, my boyfriend Abel and my publishing counselor Denis's support has made the once-daunting task that much more feasible. This support network has been essential and demonstrates the importance of not facing challenges in isolation.

It is my hope that this book will serve as a catalyst for this envisioned community, carrying forward the same mission. My goal is to provide training programs, deliver speeches, and organize retreats through this platform. The aim is straightforward yet multi-faceted: to promote connection, understanding, and empowerment, ultimately overcoming the isolation that often comes with traumatic experiences.

Me and my family

Anette and me

Raymond and me

CONCLUSION
Embracing Resilience

The path I have traveled has been filled with traumatic experiences, but it has also been a story of both resilience and the power that arises when we face our challenges directly. I started to write this book in order to unravel the web of fear, despair, and injustice that had consumed me for years. However, once the ink had dried, it became my hope that it will transform into a larger story that will connect with the collective hardships of others.

As I recount the intricacies of my harrowing experience, the underlying message echoes loud and clear: **no one has to walk this path alone**. Our shared struggles connect us in ways that words cannot express. With every page turned, we move closer and closer to breaking down the isolating walls that trauma inevitably builds.

I thank you for allowing me to take you on a journey through my trauma, and would ask that you show compassion to all those who are currently struggling in silence, too afraid to begin their own journey of healing. I urge you to not only read these words but to take them with you and make a real difference in the world.

As the last paragraph folds into the final words, I am filled with the hope that these words serve as both a remedy for wounds and a rallying cry for a future where no one has to walk alone. The story continues, and with each step forward, we ourselves will collectively write the narrative of triumph over trauma, of resilience in the face of despair, and of a future where our shared humanity transcends all the echoes of the past.

You might be wondering, where Rick is today? To be honest, I am not sure. But I have decided that he is not in control of my future. As I told you at the beginning of my book, I am just your average girl next door. I could be the girl at the check-out where you buy your groceries every week, or the waitress who serves you and your friends a round of drinks on a night out. My point is that you wouldn't look at me twice if we passed in the streets, and that is the point. Rick is very much the same. He could be the guy you stand next to on a bus or say hello to on your way to work every day. If you saw him on the street you would never think that he was capable of some of the things he has done. When I reflect upon events, I have come to realise that, in a way, Rick was also a victim of his actions, however I doubt I will ever forgive him for what he did. He is out of mind and out of sight now and it is my full intention to keep it that way.

To those who lent their unwavering support throughout this process, to Denis and Abel for their guidance, and to my family and friends for being there for me—I extend my deepest gratitude. This book is not just mine; it is ours, a collective endeavor to illuminate the shadows, break the silence, and pave the way for a future where resilience triumphs over adversity.

Resources

If you or someone you know is a victim of stalking, please know that you are not alone and that there is help available. In addition to the guidance and support offered within these pages, I have compiled a comprehensive list of resources to aid in your journey towards safety and healing. From self-assessments, checklists, and safety plans, to informative websites, support groups, crisis hotlines, and legal resources, the following pages offer a wealth of trusted and vetted tools to help you navigate the complex and often frightening experience of stalking. Whether you are seeking emotional support, practical advice, or professional assistance, I hope that these resources will serve as a beacon of hope and a reminder that you deserve to be safe and free from harm.

Stalking, characterized by a pattern of repeated, unwanted attention, harassment, or contact, is a crime that recognizes no borders. A United Nations' global survey reveals a concerning statistic: around 1 in 3 women worldwide have experienced physical or sexual intimate partner violence or non-partner sexual violence, often accompanied by stalking.

Stalking leaves a lasting impact, and it is not unique to any country or culture. In the United States, the Centers for Disease Control and Prevention (CDC) reports that nearly 1 in 6 women and 1 in 17 men have experienced stalking at some point in their lives. A study by the European Institute for Gender Equality reveals that 18% of women in the European Union have encountered stalking since the age of 15. In the UK, that number is 21%. These sobering statistics serve as the backdrop against which my personal journey unfolds.

Through the sharing of my own personal experience, I hope to expose the urgent nature of this crisis. My story reflects the harsh experiences of victims everywhere, from invasion of personal space to cyberstalking.

This is not a work of fiction; rather, it is a raw and unfiltered account based on my lived experiences—a woman who, like countless others, found herself ensnared in the suffocating clutches of a stalker. The objective extends beyond sharing a deeply personal journey; it is a call to illuminate a crisis that thrives in the shadows of silence.

I hope this jorney helps you to develop an insight and understanding of the feelings & emotions that I and so many others have been through, and many more around the world are going through. Let us recognize the global urgency to confront this issue head-on and dismantle the barriers that shroud it in secrecy. It is my hope that my own personal account will serve as a call to action, urging us to collectively confront the reality that stalking is not confined by social or geographic boundaries but tears through the lives of individuals across the globe.

With that being said, I would like to thank you for taking the time to acknowledge and read my book, and I hope that if you or anyone you know and love is or has been affected by stalking, that through the pages of this book you find the strength to fight and carry on as I did.

Likelihood that you are being/have been stalked – Self-Assessment

Instructions: The following is a self-assessment questionnaire with 20 questions to help determine the likelihood that you are being or have been stalked. Please answer each question honestly and to the best of your knowledge.

Question	Yes	No
Have you noticed someone frequently following or watching you?		
Do you receive unwanted phone calls, text messages, or emails from someone?		
Have you found evidence of someone entering your home or property without permission?		
Do you often see the same person in places you frequent, such as your workplace or neighborhood, who has no reason to be there?		
Have you received unsolicited gifts or packages from someone you do not know or have a relationship with?		
Do you feel constantly anxious or on edge, fearing that someone is watching or monitoring you?		

Question	Yes	No
Have you noticed signs of tampering with your personal belongings, such as your car, computer, or personal documents?		
Do you frequently receive messages or comments on social media or online platforms that make you uncomfortable or fearful?		
Have you noticed any unusual behavior from someone you know, such as excessive interest in your personal life or activities?		
Do you feel like your privacy has been invaded, even in your own home?		
Have you experienced any form of harassment or intimidation from someone, either in person or online?		
Do you often change your routines or habits to avoid encountering a specific person?		
Have you received any threats or warnings from someone, either directly or indirectly?		
Do you feel like you are constantly being watched or monitored, even when there is no evidence to support it?		
Have you noticed any unusual or suspicious activity around your home or workplace?		
Do you feel like your personal information or private conversations have been accessed or shared without your consent?		
Have you experienced any form of physical assault or violence from someone?		
Do you feel like your personal boundaries have been violated by someone?		
Have you sought help or support from friends, family, or authorities regarding your concerns about being stalked?		
Do you have a gut feeling or intuition that someone is stalking you, even if you cannot provide concrete evidence?		
Totals		

Please note that this self-assessment questionnaire is not a definitive diagnosis, but it can help you evaluate your situation and determine if further action or support is needed. If you answered "yes" to multiple questions or have serious concerns about your safety, it is highly recommended to seek professional help or contact local authorities for assistance.

Safety Plan for Victims of Stalking

General Safety Plan:

1. **Assess Your Safety**
   - Evaluate your surroundings and potential risks.
   - Identify safe places and escape routes.

2. **Establish a Support System**
   - Share your situation with trusted friends, family, or colleagues.
   - Create a network of reliable individuals who can provide emotional support.

3. **Inform Local Authorities**
   - Report the stalking incidents to the police.
   - Provide them with detailed information and any evidence you may have.

4. **Obtain a Restraining Order**
   - Consult with legal professionals to obtain a restraining order against the stalker.
   - Keep a copy of the order accessible at all times.

5. **Vary Your Routine**
   - Change your daily routine and routes to avoid predictability.
   - Be cautious about sharing your schedule online or with others.

6. **Enhance Home Security**
   - Install security systems, change locks, and secure windows.
   - Consider obtaining a security camera for added protection.

7. **Train for Self-Defense**
   - Enroll in self-defense classes to enhance personal safety skills.

- Carry personal safety devices if legally permitted. (pepper/bear spray, etc.)

8. **Safety Apps**
   - Download and use safety apps that allow quick communication with trusted contacts or authorities.

9. **Keep Emergency Contacts Handy**
   - Save emergency numbers on your phone and keep them easily accessible.
   - Share your location with trusted contacts when needed.

10. **Secure Personal Information**
    - Be cautious about sharing personal information online and offline.
    - Update passwords regularly and use strong, unique combinations.

11. **Emergency Bag**
    - Prepare an emergency bag with essential items such as identification, medications, and important documents.
    - Keep it easily accessible in case of a sudden need to leave.

Mobile Phone and Social Media Safety Plan:

Mobile Phone and Social Media Security Plan
Created in collaboration with Mia Landsem (Security Expert, Author and Speaker) Mialandsem.no

1. **Secure Your Mobile Phone**
   - Set a strong password, PIN, or pattern lock on your phone.
   - Enable biometric authentication (fingerprint, face recognition) if available.
   - Ensure that only you have physical access to your mobile and other devices.

2. **Check Privacy Settings**
   - Regularly review and update privacy settings on your social media accounts.
   - Limit the information visible to the public and adjust settings for friend requests and messages.

SAFETY PLAN FOR VICTIMS OF STALKING

3. **Be Mindful of Location Services**
   - Turn off location services for social media apps and adjust phone settings to limit location sharing.
   - Do not post where you are at in real time, if you are in a nice cafe, you can post the picture after you have left.

4. **Regularly Change Passwords**
   - Change passwords for email, social media, and other online accounts frequently.
   - Ensure that passwords have nothing to do with you i.e., pet names, date of birth, anniversary etc.
   - Use unique, strong passwords for each account.
   - Do not share passwords and code locks for mobile and other devices.

5. **Enable Two-Factor Authentication (2FA)**
   - Activate 2FA for added security on all accounts, especially those linked to social media and email.

6. **Review App Permissions**
   - Regularly review the permissions granted to apps on your phone.
   - Remove unnecessary app permissions that may compromise your privacy.

7. **Screen Calls and Messages**
   - Avoid answering calls or messages from unknown numbers.
   - Block and report harassing or threatening calls and messages.

8. **Use a Secondary Phone Number**
   - Consider using a secondary phone number for public activities or online interactions.
   - Apps like Google Voice or secondary SIM cards can provide an additional layer of privacy.
   - Ensure that passwords have nothing to do with you i.e., pet names, date of birth, anniversary etc."

9. **Document and Save Evidence (see Stalker Harassment Evidence Gathering Checklist on page 89 of this book)**

10. **Educate Yourself on Cybersecurity**
    - Stay informed about cybersecurity best practices.
    - Learn about phishing attempts, scams, and how to recognize and avoid them.

11. **Limit Social Media Presence**
    - Consider reducing your online presence temporarily or limiting the amount of personal information shared.
    - Be cautious about posting real-time updates or check-ins.

12. **Create a Trusted Contacts List**
    - Share your situation with close friends and family.
    - Provide them with a list of trusted contacts who can verify information and confirm your safety.

13. **Plan Emergency Communication**
    - Establish a code word or phrase with trusted individuals to signal that you are in immediate danger.
    - Ensure they are aware of the significance and can act swiftly.

14. **Screen Social Media Connections**
    - Regularly review your social media connections and remove unfamiliar or suspicious individuals.
    - Adjust settings to approve tags and mentions before they appear on your profile.

15. **Report to Platforms**
    - Report the stalker to the respective social media platforms.
    - Familiarize yourself with each platform's reporting mechanisms and follow their procedures.

16. **Inform Local Authorities**
    - Keep local law enforcement informed about the stalking situation.
    - Provide them with evidence and updates regularly.

17. **Seek Professional Guidance**
    - Consult with cybersecurity professionals if you suspect your online accounts have been compromised.
    - Reach out to local domestic violence hotlines for advice tailored to your situation.

18. **Trust Your Instincts**
    - If you feel unsafe or suspect any compromise, take immediate action.
    - Adjust your social media and mobile phone settings based on the evolving situation.

Remember, your safety plan should be dynamic and adapt to changes in your circumstances. Regularly reassess your plan and seek support from professionals and trusted contacts.

Stalker Harassment Evidence Gathering Checklist:

Dealing with a stalker is a serious and distressing situation. Properly documenting and collecting evidence is crucial for law enforcement to take appropriate action. Use this checklist to ensure you gather comprehensive evidence for reporting stalking incidents to the police:

I. **Stalking Incidents Documentation:**

Incident Log
- Create a detailed incident log for each stalking event.
- Include date, time, location, description of the incident, and any potential witnesses.

Photos or Videos
- Document any signs of stalking such as strangers near your residence or workplace.
- Capture screenshots of online harassment or messages.

II. **Communication Records:**

Call Logs
- Maintain a record of all phone calls received from the stalker.
- Include date, time, and duration of each call.

Text Messages and Emails
- Save all text messages, emails, and online communication.
- Note date, time, and content of each message.

III. **Social Media Evidence:**

Screenshots
- Take screenshots of any suspicious or harassing posts, messages, or interactions on social media platforms.
- Include usernames and timestamps.

IV. Physical Evidence:

Mail or Packages
- Keep envelopes, packages, or any physical items received from the stalker.
- Note dates of receipt.

V. Witness Statements:

Witness Information
- Collect contact information for any witnesses to stalking incidents.
- Encourage them to provide statements to law enforcement.

VI. Online Activity:

IP Addresses
- Note IP addresses associated with suspicious emails or messages.
- Report to the police to aid in tracking the stalker's online activity.

Device Information
- Document details of any suspicious devices used by the stalker.
- Include make, model, and any identifiable markings.

VII. Restraining Orders or Legal Documentation:

- Previous Reports or Restraining Orders
- Include any previous reports filed with the police.
- Provide copies of existing restraining orders or legal documentation.

VIII. Personal Safety Measures:

Home Security
- Install or upgrade home security systems, including cameras and alarms.
- Document any attempts of forced entry or tampering.

Self-Defense Measures
- Seek professional advice on self-defense measures.
- Document any instances where you felt physically threatened.

IX. Emotional Impact:

Mental Health Documentation
- Keep records of any impact on mental health.
- Seek professional support and documentation if needed.

X. Reporting to Law Enforcement:

Police Reports
- File a comprehensive police report detailing all collected evidence.
- Provide all documentation, ensuring nothing is omitted.

Follow-Up
- Regularly follow up with law enforcement on the progress of the case.
- Provide any additional evidence as it becomes available.

Remember, it's crucial to prioritize personal safety throughout this process. If you feel threatened or endangered at any point, contact the authorities immediately. This checklist aims to provide a thorough framework for evidence collection, enhancing the chances of a successful intervention by law enforcement.

Online Stalker Victim Resources

Here are online resources that can provide assistance and support for victims of stalkers:

- National Stalking Helpline (UK) – Provides advice and support for victims of stalking. Website: https://www.suzylamplugh.org/
- National Center for Victims of Crime (USA) – Offers resources and support for victims of stalking. Website: https://victimsofcrime.org/
- Stalking Resource Center – Provides information, resources, and support for victims of stalking. Website: https://www.stalkingawareness.org/
- National Domestic Violence Hotline (USA) – Offers support and resources for victims of stalking and domestic violence. Website: https://www.thehotline.org/
- Victim Support (UK) – Provides emotional support, information, and practical help for victims of stalking. Website: https://www.victimsupport.org.uk/
- Cyber Civil Rights Initiative – Provides resources and support for victims of online harassment and cyberstalking. Website: https://www.cybercivilrights.org/
- National Network to End Domestic Violence (USA) – Provides resources and support for victims of stalking and domestic violence. Website: https://nnedv.org/
- Paladin National Stalking Advocacy Service (UK) – Offers advice, support, and advocacy for victims of stalking. Website: https://paladinservice.co.uk/
- Victim Connect Resource Center (USA) – Provides information, referrals, and support for all types of crime victims, including stalking. Website: https://victimconnect.org/

- Women's Aid (UK) – Offers support and resources for women experiencing stalking and domestic violence. Website: https://www.womensaid.org.uk/

- Stalking Helpline (Australia) – Provides support and advice for victims of stalking in Australia. Website: https://www.1800respect.org.au/

- National Organization for Victim Assistance (USA) – Offers resources, support, and advocacy for victims of stalking and other crimes. Website: https://www.trynova.org/

- Men's Advice Line (UK) – Offers support and advice for male victims of stalking and domestic abuse. Website: https://mensadviceline.org.uk/

- Crime Victim Services – A directory of local victim service providers that can assist victims of stalking. Website: https://www.crimevictimservices.org/

- Please note that these resources are not ranked in any particular order, and it is important to choose the ones that are most relevant to your situation and location.

Mia Landsem (Security expert, author and speaker)

"The book is important and focuses on a topic that affects many more people than you might think. There are many who live in fear without being heard or without getting the help they deserve."

About the upcoming book by Otto Heutling:
FemPowerment - The Future of Women's Self Defense

Redefining Women's Self Defense - it's about freedom, not fear

Self-defense is about much more than ninja moves... it's about personal empowerment - not only when in danger, but always

I had trained in martial arts for more than 35 years and had my own martial arts school in Sydney, Australia for 20 years as part of an organization whose slogan was 'The Science of Self Defense'. Even though the style itself was effective, it still didn't work for everyone. Not everyone had the same talent, the will, the confidence, the physical prerequisites, the time or the desire.

But if this was about self-defense, was it really about the fighting moves or simply about safety? I learned over the years that there are other things that laid a more important and effective foundation to self-defense: Why were these situations occurring? How could you recognize them early on? How could you prevent them from happening?

The biggest problem is not the lack of fighting skills, but the lack of understanding of the problem itself. The book FemPowerment changes that.

Making sense of self-defense

FemPowerment describes a completely unique way of doing self-defense. **FemPowerment helps women step back into their inherent power**. The shared knowledge helps women deal with problems, big or small, dangerous or not and consequently feel safe and free again.

Insecurity comes from uncertainty. In this book you will learn straight forward principles that any woman can apply regardless of the situation, old or young, fit or not. **It teaches you never to become a victim**.

PHASE 1: **ENERGY**
TOOL: **CONFIDENCE**

PHASE 2: **AWARENESS**
TOOL: **INTUITION**

PROJECT
FEMPOWERMENT

PHASE 4: **FIGHTING**
TOOL: **DETERMINATION**

PHASE 3: **BOUNDARIES**
TOOL: **ASSERTIVENESS**

Fighting skills are only a smaller part of a much more holistic self-defense model. **It's about learning to trust your intuition (to help you recognize danger early), setting effective boundaries (to de-escalate danger preemptively), building of confidence, determination and a whole new way of thinking**. In truth, this is what is needed to deal with any kind of unwanted situation and even to prevent it completely.

Ironically, these are the traits needed to be able to apply fighting techniques in the first place, more so than the techniques themselves, and having those traits makes it less and less likely that those techniques are needed at all. **More so than dealing with danger, it helps women live every aspect of their lives with more control and freedom - be it at home, at work, their social lives or in their communities**.

You will never see self-defense or your safety the same way again!

To learn about more about the book and Project FemPowerment go to:
www.projectfempowerment.com

Or for a straight forward and concise video course go to:
www.fempowermentessentials.com

Marion Langli's goal is to provide training programs, deliver speeches, and organize retreats as an extension of her book "**Stalked – My story of Terror and Triumph.**" Her aim is straightforward yet deep: to promote connection, understanding, and empowerment, ultimately overcoming the isolation that often comes with traumatic experiences. Marion is open to potential partnerships to positively impact more people around the globe.

For more information about exploring how Marion Langli can help your organization, clients or members please contact:

Website: https://reachabel.com/the-stalked-book/
Email: marion@reachabel.com
LinkedIn: http://www.linkedin.com/MarionLangli

www.ingramcontent.com/pod-product-compliance
Lightning Source LLC
Chambersburg PA
CBHW070545170426
43200CB00011B/2558